FITTER, FASTER, FUNNIER OLYMPICS!

Published 2012 by
A & C Black, an imprint of
Bloomsbury Publishing Plc
50 Bedford Square, London, WC1B 3DP

www.acblack.com
www.bloomsbury.com
ISBN 978-1-4081-6558-4

Printed and bound in Great Britain by CPI Cox and Wyman,
Reading, RG1 8EX

IMPORTANT:

When throwing heavy (or sharp) things around,
(or yourself for that matter), it is essential that
you follow proper safety precautions, and receive
proper supervision and instructions from a
trained professional or teacher.

FITTER, FASTER, FUNNIER OLYMPICS!

Michael Cox

Illustrated by Steve May

A & C Black • London

CONTENTS

So What's So Funny About the Olympics?   6-7

1: The Ancient Olympics

Where Did It Begin?   8-9
Grisly Greek Grapplers   10-11
How Well Do You Know Your Ancient Olympics?   12-13
A Tale of Two Statues   14-15

2: The Modern Olympics

They're Back *and* A Mind-Boggling Olympic Timeline   16-23
Are You Cut Out to be a Medal-Winning Olympic Athlete?   24-27
How Did You Score?   28-29
Ten Ways to Fit Olympic Training into Your Daily Routine   30-31
Some Useful Advice to Would-Be Olympians   32-35

3: Just Horsing Around

How to Be an Olympic Medal-Winning Show Jumper   36-37
Essential Show Jumping Tips   38-39
A Hugely Heroic Horseman   40-41

4: Fight!

Getting it Out of Your System   42-43
How to Be an Olympic Wrestler   44-45
Let's Wrestle: What You Need   46-47
Olympics Wrestlers: Know Your Moves   48-49

5: Bike Dreams

Pedal for a Medal   50-51
How Well Do You Know Your BMX Stunts?   52-53

6: Half Time: What Happened Next?   54-57

7: Stretch Yourself
Bendy, Bouncy, Brilliant!   58-59
How Well Do You Know Your Olympic Gymnastic Moves?   60-61

8: The 'Athlons
Tri', Pent', Hept' and Dec' (but no Ant)   62-63
The Triathlon: Be Prepared!   64-65
Training for Transitions   66-69

9: Chucking Stuff and Jumping Over Things
Track and Field Events   70-71
How to Throw the Olympic Hammer   72-75
Throwing the Javelin   76-77
The Pole Vault   78-81

10: Run for Your Life
Olympic Running   82-83
The Distance Races   84-85
The Marathon *and* Long-Distance Jogging Jargon Quiz   86-89
The Mind-Boggling St Louis Marathon of 1904   90-91

11: The Really Sweaty Stuff
Weightlifting   92-93
Ball Games   94-95
Three Essential Skills for Aspiring Olympic Footballers   96-97

12: Completely Batty!
Bat and Ball Games... Where Did They Begin?   98-100
The Olympic Table Tennis Test   101-103

13: Just Splashing Around
Don't Be a Drip, Get Wet!   104-107
How to Be a Medal-Winning Olympic Swimmer   108-109
Super-Slow Olympic Hero!   110-111
Tips for Olympic Swimmers   112-113
What Not to Do at an Olympic Swimming Event   114-115

14: The "Do-it-Yourself" Olympics   116-123

Glossary   124-126
Further Information   127
Index   128

So What's So Funny About The Olympics?

We all know that the Olympics are an awe-inspiring sporting spectacle in which world-class athletes battle for glory. But did you know that they're also the setting for absolutely hundreds of weird, wonderful and wildly hilarious moments! In the awesomely agile, ferociously fleet-footed and superbly supple pages of this book, you will discover...

Who took over 54 years to finish his Olympic marathon?

Where Olympic swimmers had to swim under and climb over rowing boats?

Why Olympic basketball players used to have to take a ladder to their matches?

How did a pair of flaming underpants get mistaken for the Olympic torch?

But that's not all!

Find out how to shine at show-jumping, win at wrestling, triumph in the triathlon, swim like a superstar and perform an Olympic medal-winning javelin throw, but NOT (for health and safety reasons), how to do these things all at once! Discover if you've got what it takes to be an Olympic superstar, by completing two incredibly insightful questionnaires, and find out how to incorporate your Olympic training into your daily life. And if all that's not enough to keep you on the edge of your grandstand seat, there are also exciting instructions on how to create your own "DIY Olympics".

IMPORTANT SAFETY NOTE: As you will notice quite quickly, a lot of the instructions in this book are somewhere between totally daft and certifiably insane. In other words they are not meant to be taken seriously. Therefore if you…

a) get your head stuck in the ceiling doing a "fliffus" on your trampoline

b) strangle yourself whilst trying to perform an Olympic medal winning "hammer throw" using a frozen chicken and piece of string

c) kebab an entire queue of people at a bus stop during your javelin practice

or do anything that is detrimental to your general health and most squishy bodily particulates, neither Michael Cox, his publishers, or his Aunty Sandra, can be held responsible / in prison / to ransom / over a barrel.

So what are you waiting for! Lace up your trainers, slip on your shorts, slap on some sun cream and strap on your heart monitor! Then it's…

ON YOUR MARKS…
GET SET… GO!

1 THE ANCIENT OLYMPICS

WHERE DID IT BEGIN?

The first ancient Olympic Games took place in Greece in 776 BC, (that's almost 3,000 years ago). They were held in the valley of Olympia, (now there's a coincidence) and happened every four years.

The stroppy Greek city-states, who were normally busy having wars and what-not, always declared a truce during the games. The events included chariot races, boxing, wrestling and marathons, and the competitors always took part in the nude, (in which case, where did the marathon runners keep their iPods?).

Partway through the games, dozens of oxen were sacrificed to Zeus (the king of all the ancient Greek gods), and in an attempt to predict the outcomes of their events, Olympic athletes examined the entrails (intestines) of the slaughtered animals (yes, it takes guts to compete in the Olympics).

TORCH AND GO!

The Olympic torch, which is carried around the host nation and into the stadium at the beginning of the modern Olympics, is said to have been inspired by an ancient Greek relay race where, instead of a baton, the runners carried burning torches. The idea was to get to the end of the race before the torch went out (or set the runners' legs on fire).

IF YOU VALUE HER LIFE, DON'T BRING YOUR WIFE!

Young unmarried girls could watch the ancient Olympics, but if married women were caught attending the games they immediately became "harried" women, closely followed by "carried" women, when they were taken to the top of nearby Mount Typaion and thrown off!

However, one woman, Kallipateira, disguised herself as a chap so she could watch her son, a boxer, compete in his event. When he won, she was so chuffed that she jumped over the barrier to congratulate him but, as she did, all her clothes fell off, (the way they do) and she was revealed to be a woman.

However, in recognition of her father, three brothers, nephew and son, who were all Olympic champions, the officials let her off the "being-thrown-off-a-mountain" bit, (and simply rolled her down a nearby railway embankment).

GRISLY GREEK GRAPPLERS

Ancient Olympic Greek wrestlers covered themselves with oil and dust to make it easier for their opponents to get hold of them. Biting, tripping and eye gouging were against the rules but punching, choking and breaking your opponent's fingers were all perfectly acceptable.

One ancient Olympic wrestler, Sostratus of Sikyon, (or "Mr Fingertips", as he was known to his fans), regularly snapped his opponents' digits to make them submit. Another ancient Greek grappler, Polydamas, was so strong that he once killed a lion with his bare hands.

On another occasion, he seized a huge bull by its foot, actually pulling off its hoof when the beast tried to escape. He also brought a fast-moving chariot to a halt simply by grabbing it with his bare hands!

In order to train for such phenomenal feats of strength, one ancient Olympic wrestler, Milo of Kroton, trained by carrying a live calf around with him every day. As the calf grew, so did his muscles, (especially his calf muscles).

BOXING CLEVER, WITH A PAINFUL BIT OF LEATHER

Instead of wearing gloves, ancient Greek boxers wrapped leather straps around their hands to protect them. The straps caused terrible damage to their opponents' faces, apart from one fleet-footed fighter, the ancient Greek boxer Melankomas of Karia.

ANCIENT GREASE!

Melankomas was so nimble that his opponents never managed to land a punch on him and he never bothered to land one on them. He simply ducked and weaved until they were completely exhausted, at which point he would be declared the winner. He never lost a match and never once hit an opponent.

How Well Do You Know Your Ancient Olympics?

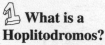

Here are some ancient Greek words from those long ago Olympics. See if you can guess the right meanings!

1 What is a Hoplitodromos?

a) a foot race in which the athletes wore armour

b) a foot race in which the athletes had to hop the entire distance

c) the lamp used to light up the hopping race, which was always held at night

2 Who or what is Nike?

a) ancient Greek name for a running shoe

b) the ancient Greek goddess of victory

c) a running shoe spike which has been worn away to nothing

3 What is a Periodonikes?

a) an Olympic race involving very old donkeys

b) the name of the man who looked after the donkeys

c) the athlete who won all of the big four running events

4 What is Pankration?
a) a martial arts event in which the contestants hit each other with frying pans
b) a "no-holds-barred" fighting event
c) small amounts of food given to athletes just before their events

5 Who or what is Pugme?
a) a very small Olympic athlete
b) an ancient Greek expression meaning, "Well, I never!"
c) the ancient Olympic boxing event

6 What is the Hippodrome?
a) the place where the hippopotamus wrestling event took place
b) a really cool and trendy competitor
c) the horse racing course

7 What is or are Dolichos?
a) tasty snacks served to ancient Greek Olympic spectators
b) a distance race of between two and a half and five kilometres
c) a nasty groin condition brought about by not changing your loincloth regularly

A TALE OF TWO STATUES

Eight episodes from the life of Theo of Theagenes, an Olympic hero and junior statue thief!

1 Little Theo liked a massive bronze statue of a god so much that he pinched it from his local market square.

2 The townsfolk wanted to execute him but, recognising his amazing physical strength, they spared his life, (and gave him a clip round the ear instead).

3 Theo became a brilliant athlete and an Olympic boxer, going on to win 1300 laurel crowns in 22 years at the Olympics and other important sporting events.

4 After Theo died, a statue was erected in his honour. But every night one his old rivals would come and "box" the statue in revenge for being thrashed by Theo so many times.

5 One night the statue fell on one of his former rivals, squashing him to death!

6 The rival's sons had the statue "tried" for murder and "sentenced to death". It was then thrown into the sea.

7 Some years later the crops failed and the local wise man told the townsfolk to bring the statue of Theo back to the town.

They did and, when the crops grew again, Theo was worshipped as a god.

THEY'RE OFF! THE END OF THE ANCIENT OLYMPICS

The Olympic Games continued for 1100 years but in AD 393 the ancient world's first-ever true spoil-sport, Roman Emperor Theodosius, banned them, saying they were disrespectful to the gods, (but added that he would rather miss the sight of all those hundreds of wobbly bare bottoms).

2 THE MODERN OLYMPICS

THEY'RE BACK!

In the late nineteenth century, a French nobleman with an enormous moustache called Baron Pierre de Coubertin (he was called that, not the moustache), decided to bring back the Olympics. As a result, the first modern Olympic Games were held in Greece in 1896. And so began a series of world-class sporting events filled with heroics, thrills, stunning achievements and spectacular silliness.

A MIND-BOGGLING MODERN OLYMPIC TIMELINE

1896
First Modern Olympic Games, Athens, Greece
Women were banned from taking part. Baron de Coubertin said they would be, "impractical, uninteresting, unaesthetic and incorrect", (what a charming and forward-thinking fellow!).

The games were opened by King George I of Greece. One French sprinter was so awestruck by the fact that his event was to be watched by royalty that he insisted on wearing gloves during his race.

Several of the competitors weren't actually official competitors at all, but people who just happened to be in Greece at the time. One of these, an Irish tennis fan called John Mary Pius Boland, not only ended up as half of the winning German doubles duo, but also won the men's singles final.

The swimming events took place in the freezing cold sea where the course was marked by hollowed-out pumpkins. Swimmers had to struggle against twelve-foot-high waves and many, having gone completely numb with cold, were hauled out of the water by rescuers in small boats.

The marathon was won by Spiridon Louis, a Greek water-carrier who walked miles every day, lugging heavy buckets of mineral water to Athens. Various rich Greeks were so delighted with Spiridon's win that they offered him free clothes, sheep, cows, barrels of wine, 900 kilograms of chocolate, tons of dosh and free haircuts for life.

One millionaire even offered Spiridon his daughter's hand in marriage. But Spiridon, who was already married, turned down all these offers, saying he would be perfectly happy with a horse and cart to make his water-carrying job a bit easier. He never ran again (but did occasionally use his new horse and cart in chariot races).

1900

Olympics, Paris, France

Only two cricket teams entered, a British team from
Devon and Somerset who thrashed the "French" team,
which was made up of staff from the British embassy.

The swimming events took place in the River Seine,
and included an obstacle race in which swimmers
had to clamber over and swim under lines of rowing boats.
Oh yes, and they also had to climb a pole!

Women could now enter the Olympics and an
American golfer, Margaret Abbott, managed to win
the Olympic gold medal for women's golf, without even
realising she was taking part!

1904

Olympics, St Louis, USA

This Olympics featured "Anthropology Days", with games for "costumed members of the uncivilized tribes", including mud fighting, tree climbing, rock throwing, pole climbing and spear throwing. An official complained that the African pygmies were "full of mischief", and that they took nothing seriously, apart from the "tree climbing".

American athlete, George Eyser won two gold, two silver, and one bronze medal at the games in gymnastics… despite having a wooden leg.

1908

Olympics, London, England

When the American tug-of-war team was beaten by the British team, composed entirely of policemen, they accused them of wearing illegal spiked boots. A rematch was held with the teams in their socks. The British "bobbies" won again.

1912

Olympics, Stockholm, Sweden

During the Olympic marathon, Japanese athlete, Shizo Kanakuri stopped for a drink offered by some people at a garden party, then got chatting to them and sort of "forgot" he was taking part in the Olympics. Full of shame at his failure to complete the marathon, he fled home to Japan without telling anyone.

In 1966 he was tracked down and offered the chance to complete the marathon. He accepted, ending up with a time of 54 years, 8 months, 6 days, 8 hours, 32 minutes and 20.3 seconds.

Also running in the 1912 Olympic marathon were South African team mates, Kennedy McArthur and Charles Gitsan. They were well ahead of the rest of the runners when Charles began to feel thirsty, so Kennedy told Charles to stop for a drink, saying he'd wait for him. The moment Charles stopped, Kennedy raced away and won the race by one minute and twenty seconds.

1920

Olympics, Antwerp, Belgium

Italian athlete Ugo Frigerio gave the conductor of the official Olympic band a list of tunes he wanted playing while he did the 3,000 metre walk event. The conductor did as he was asked and Frigerio "conducted" the band as he walked. He also won the race.

1924

Olympics, Paris, France

Incredibly, the athletes running the Olympic marathon were waited on by servants who offered them wine and refreshments. Another sausage, sir?

1936

Olympics, Berlin, Germany

A female German athlete, Dora Ratjen, who competed in the high jump, was later discovered to be a male German waiter called Hermann. When asked why he had posed as a woman to enter the event, Hermann is reported to have claimed that the Nazis had forced him to do it for the glory of Germany, adding, "For three years I lived the life of a girl. It was most dull."

 Name that tune! During the Berlin Olympics, the German national anthem was played 400 times.

1948

Olympics, London, England

The English national anthem was played only three times during the games.

1956

Olympics, Melbourne, Australia

Due to extreme temperatures, over 225 people collapsed with heat exhaustion during the opening ceremony.

Weightlifter, Charles Vinci discovered that he was 200 grams too heavy to qualify for his event just 15 minutes before the weigh-in. So he cut off all his hair, managed to qualify, and went on to win a gold medal.

1960

Olympics, Rome, Italy

Don Thompson, a race walker, was worried about the extreme Italian heat and humidity he would have to cope with during his race. So he filled a room in his house with heaters and boiling kettles and trained in this "homemade sauna". And it paid off! Despite the heat, he won the 50,000 metres walk.

Sir Ludwig Guttman, a neurologist who worked with World War II veterans with spinal injuries, brought 400 wheelchair athletes to compete in the Olympic games. And so the modern Parallel Olympics, or "Paralympics", were born.

1964

Tokyo Olympics:
Two cyclists balanced on their bikes, totally motionless...
for a mind-boggling 22 minutes! The wheels on the bikes
go, err... nowhere!

1976

Olympics, Toronto, Canada
Arnie Boldt, a Canadian with only one leg, jumped a
mind-boggling 1.86 metres during the Paralympics high
jumping event.

1992

Olympics, Barcelona, Spain
Solo synchronised swimming was an official event.

DiD YOU KNOW?

Between 1912 and 1952, architecture,
literature, music, painting and sculpture
were all Olympic events, the theme
being "sport-inspired". Imagine winning
Olympic gold for writing a haiku (a very
short poem), or getting a bronze medal
for your "football" sculpting skills!

Are You Cut Out To Be a Medal-Winning Olympic Athlete?

Take this short test and find out!

Part A: Your Athletic Abilities

1 Is your body...
a) wedge-shaped
b) pear-shaped
c) pumpkin-shaped

2 When faced with a steep hill to climb, do you...
a) sprint up it, feeling energetic and confident
b) walk up it slowly, making frequent stops to catch your breath
c) call for a taxi

3 Would you describe your shoulders as...
a) broad and muscular
b) a little on the skinny side
c) what shoulders?

4 On doing a forward roll, do you...
a) perform it nimbly and gracefully
b) do it cautiously and painfully
c) become so entangled by your own limbs that the emergency services have to be called to unravel you

5 **Would you describe yourself as...**
a) lithe and spritely
b) a bit clumsy
c) having all the agility and dexterity of a dead slug

6 **When you go to hit a ball with a bat, do you...**
a) strike it confidently and squarely
b) lash out at it wildly
c) miss it completely and smash yourself in the face

7 **When touching your toes do you...**
a) reach them easily
b) struggle a bit
c) find it completely impossible as you're not actually able to see them

8 **If you accidentally scratch yourself, do you...**
a) think nothing of it
b) put a plaster on it
c) scream hysterically then call an ambulance

9 **When teams are being picked for games, do the choosers...**
a) fight over which one of them is to get you on their side
b) let you pick which team you want to be on because you're all mates
c) have to bribe you to play to even out the sides with the promise to return your book... after the game!

10 **If someone throws a ball at you, do you...**
a) catch it smoothly and confidently then throw it back to them
b) catch it but then fumble it and drop it
c) curl up like a terrified hedgehog, whimpering pitifully

PART B: YOUR ATTITUDE

1 Would you describe yourself as...
a) a supremely confident winner (almost superhuman, actually)
b) someone who always tries their best but does have the occasional setback
c) not in the slightest bit bothered about being "top banana"

2 If you come last in a sporting event, do you feel...
a) furious with yourself and determined to do better next time
b) slightly disappointed, but that's OK
c) absolutely fine because you know your talents lie elsewhere

3 When entering a room full of strangers do you...
a) stride in confidently and introduce yourself to one and all
b) walk in, smiling shyly
c) wander in, lost in thoughts of sub-atomic particles and the "Meaning of Life"

4 If you see brightly coloured clothing with writing or numbers on it, do you...
a) feel very excited and quiver all over
b) feel a bit sorry for the sort of people who wear those things
c) feel inspired to paint an abstract masterpiece in the style of Picasso

5 If people stare at you in the street, do you...
a) wave and smile then break into a stunning dance routine
b) happily stare back
c) not notice, because you're too busy working out the square root of 53

6 Would you prefer to...

a) run around shouting a lot

b) watch other people running around and shouting a lot

c) play a killer guitar solo in front of thousands of adoring fans

7 Faced with a sporting challenge, do you...

a) prepare confidently and assertively

b) practice a bit and hope for the best

c) make for the nearest bookshop

8 Do you like to wear clothes which...

a) make you look lithe, powerful and athletic

b) make you look fashionable

c) make you look mysterious and "arty"

9 When people begin talking about sport, do you...

a) join in making knowledgeable contributions

b) nod enthusiastically even though you're not all that sure what they're on about

c) enter an imaginary world inhabited by werewolves, vampires and other strange and wonderful stuff

10 On wet, cold and windy outdoor games days, do you...

a) think, "Great! Another test for my limitless courage and stamina!"

b) wear three PE kits and make the best of it

c) forge a "sick note" from your parents saying you've just contracted "Wobblus Peggies Pilkitonia" or "Pilkington's Wobbly Leg Syndrome" as it's more commonly known.

So how do you think you measure up to the idea of a perfect Olympic competitor? Turn the page and find out!

How Did You Score?

Work out how many times you answered A, how many times you answered B, and how many times you answered C. Then read your results below:

If you answered mainly A
It sounds like you've got what it takes to be an Olympic medal winner. You're not only confident, courageous, talented and superbly fit, but you're also able to take setbacks (and day-glow sportswear) in your stride.

If you answered mainly B
With a little effort and training you'll enjoy a range of sports as leisure activities, and have a great time! But training for the Olympics is a completely different kettle of fish, so unless you're prepared to go the extra mile, you'll be much better off getting your thrills by watching the games.

If you answered mainly C
It sounds like intense physical activity, garish sportswear and shouting just aren't your cup of tea. So you're never going to be an Olympic champion (and probably aren't bothered anyway). However, having such an enquiring and perceptive mind, this won't stop you enjoying this book, or even the Olympics themselves!

An Encouraging Story for Struggling Would-Be Olympians

When Toshiyuki Sakata was eighteen, he weighed only 50 kilograms and was just 172 centimetres tall. But Toshiyuki wasn't at all happy with his "slight" physique. In his own words, he wanted to "look as good as the other guys".

So he began lifting weights. After lots of hard work, true grit and determination, Toshiyuki miraculously transformed himself into a mean-looking 177 centimetres and 127 kilograms of solid muscle!

Then he went on to win a silver medal for weightlifting in the 1948 London Olympics. You may have seen, Toshiyuki. He plays tough guy, Oddjob, in the James Bond film, Goldfinger. How's that for an inspiring Olympic story!

Ten Ways to Fit Olympic Training Into Your Daily Routine

1 Strength: Don't offer to "see" old ladies across the road. Offer to "carry" old ladies across the road. Preferably, as many as you possibly can at once.

2 Speed: If you find yourself running for the bus, forget actually getting on the bus! Simply whiz past it then attempt to beat it to the next bus stop.

3 Endurance: Ask your local mechanic to knock you up a human-sized hamster wheel, then have it linked to an electric battery. Not only will you get fit, you'll save your parents a fortune in lighting bills.

4 Determination: Have secret compartments stitched into the linings of all your clothes and fill them with really heavy things like sand and ball bearings. This will make everyday activities such as walking around or making a sandwich that little bit more challenging.

5 Skill: If your route to school follows a local canal or river, why not swim to and from school every day.

6 Technique: As an essential part of training for the hurdles, try "hedge-hopping" every front garden in your street, (if some of these gardens contain ferocious dogs, it may encourage you to break records you never imagined possible).

7 Agility: When you're on your way to the shops, instead of walking, consider hopping, cartwheeling, somersaulting or walking on your hands.

8 Power: The next time your family is planning a trip out in the car, offer to push the car to its intended destination, with your entire family in it. Not only will this increase your strength, you'll save the environment too!

9 Competitiveness: Compete against yourself in everything you do, timing things like how long it takes you to get dressed, brush your teeth, make a cup of tea and answer the phone. Then try to beat your records.

10 Stamina: Take the stairs two at a time, then three at a time, then four at a time, building up your skill and stamina until you are able take the whole staircase in one giant leap!

SOME USEFUL ADVICE TO WOULD-BE OLYMPIANS

REMEMBER YOUR KIT

Iranian boxer Ali Kazemi was disqualified from the 1992 Barcelona Olympics when he forget to bring his boxing gloves with him!

EAT WELL, BUT NOT TOO WELL

The ancient Greek Olympic champion wrestler, Milon of Kroton, (yes, him again), was said to have eaten a whole calf before one match. He, in turn, was later eaten by wild animals when his hands became trapped in a tree trunk he was trying to split.

DON'T TRY TO EAT YOUR OPPONENT

French boxer, Roger Brousse, was declared the winner at the end of a match at the 1924 Paris Olympics. However, when his opponent, Henry Mallin, showed officials his chest, the decision was reversed. During the match, Henry had been repeatedly bitten by Roger and his chest was covered with the teeth marks to prove it.

DON'T OVERDO THE SUNSCREEN

Before starting out on the 1912 Stockholm Olympic marathon, Portuguese runner Francisco Lazaro slathered himself with wax to prevent sunburn. This was not a good idea. Francisco dropped dead after running 29 kilometres. The wax had prevented sweat from leaving his body, resulting in a chemical imbalance that killed him.

DON'T SHOW OFF

At the award ceremony at the 1904 Olympics, men's golf champion, George Lyon, walked up to the officials on his hands to receive his trophy.

ALWAYS MAKE SURE YOU'RE PROPERLY DRESSED

At the 1948 London Olympics, just before the start of 100 metre backstroke race, a competitor from Pakistan removed his dressing gown only to discover that he'd forgotten to put on his trunks. Despite jumping into the water to hide his embarrassment, he was disqualified.

DON'T FRIGHTEN THE JUDGES IN ORDER TO WIN

At the Olympics in AD 66, the Roman Emperor Nero won every single event he entered. This may have had something to do with the fact that he was accompanied by 5,000 heavily armed bodyguards.

DON'T TAKE ANYTHING FOR GRANTED

Just after eating an enormous lunch, Joseph Guillemot was told that his 10,000 metre race at the 1920 Antwerp Olympics had been brought forward by three hours. He not only finished the race, but actually came second. He was then immediately sick all over the winner's running shoes.

KEEP YOUR COOL

After losing to Germany at the 1932 Los Angeles Olympics, the Brazilian water polo team leapt out of the pool and attacked the referee, finally chasing him out of the stadium.

AVOID FALSE STARTS

Runners who were founding guilty of making false starts at the ancient Greek Olympics were soundly whipped by officials called alytes. Ouch!

OLYMPIC SIZZLER!

Jamaican sprinter, "fastest man in the world" and three-time Olympic Gold medal winner, Usain Bolt, said he included "eating chicken nuggets" and "watching TV" as part of his training.

3 JUST HORSING AROUND

HOW TO BE AN OLYMPIC MEDAL-WINNING SHOW JUMPER

There are three sorts of Olympic equestrian (horse-related) events.

Dressage: where you and your horse just sort of "strut your stuff" in front of the judges.

Show jumping: which tests the ability of you and your horse to jump over 12 to 14 obstacles inside a riding arena, preferably together.

Eventing: which involves the above two, plus a cross-country race including lots of obstacles such as steep banks and water splashes.

TO BE A SHOW JUMPER, YOU WILL NEED...

1 Courage, skill and nerves of steel.

2 A horse and saddle. You could try galloping around the arena astride a broomstick, clothes horse, or your best friend, but you'd look very silly and probably be disqualified quite quickly.

3 An equestrian outfit, including...
a) White horse jumping breeches, these are for you to wear, not your horse.
b) A safety riding hat and riding boots, motor cycle crash helmet and cowboy boots are not acceptable.
c) A little red riding jacket (however a matching "little red riding hood" is not necessary).

4 If you have long hair you must tie it back in a pony-tail. That's a hairstyle, (do not try and tie your hair to your pony's tail).

CHOOSING YOUR HORSE

1 The best sort of horse for Olympic show jumping is one with a leg at each corner, the other sort tend to fall over quite a lot.

2 Do not choose a Shire horse, wild mustang, seaside donkey or Shetland pony for your Olympic show jumping debut. They will only disappoint.

3 Choose a fit-looking horse with an intelligent face and big bright eyes.

ESSENTIAL
SHOW JUMPING TIPS

1 Make sure your horse has been to the toilet before entering the ring.

2 Be aware that your horse may suddenly "take a fancy" to one of the other competing horses. This could be very embarrassing, especially if you happen to be on it at the time.

3 Your goal is for you and your horse to jump cleanly (i.e. without bashing anything) over the obstacles in as short a time as possible. The course itself includes all sorts of twists and turns which will test you and your horse to your limits.

4 The obstacles include double fences, gates, water jumps, (water slides, high wires and caged tigers)! If your horse touches one of these obstacles, a penalty is given against you.

5 If your horse refuses to jump an obstacle you will also be penalised.

6 A bell will ring to tell you things like when to enter the arena, if you've been eliminated, when your time is up, (or that it's playtime).

ESSENTIAL
SHOW JUMPING DON'TS

DO NOT...

1 Attempt to "limbo dance" your horse under a jump.

2 Lower a jump so that your horse can step over it.

3 Dangle a carrot in front of your horse's nose to encourage it over jumps.

4 Show off by performing "handbrake turns" on your horse.

5 "Carry" your horse over jumps.

6 Reverse your horse over jumps.

7 Threaten your horse with being turned into cat food if it refuses to jump.

DID YOU KNOW?

When his horse refused to leap over one of the jumps at the 1968 Mexico Olympics three times in a row, German rider, Hans-Jurgen Todt got so angry with it that he had to be dragged away from the arena by officials.

A Hugely Heroic Horseman

When the Olympics were held in Berlin in 1936, the German government were desperate to prove their country's power and strength to the rest of the world.

When it came to the horse riding events, they were not disappointed. During the equestrian cross country event, despite falling from his horse and pulling his left arm out of its socket, German Lieutenant Konrad Freiherr von Wagenheim remounted and managed the 32 remaining obstacles faultlessly.

The next day, at the show jumping final, Konrad reappeared before an expectant crowd of 100,000 spectators with his arm in a sling. With the "home crowd" willing him on, he was soon galloping his mount (a horse who was called Kurfurst) towards a double obstacle.

But then… disaster struck! As Konrad tried to rein him in, Kurfurst reared up and toppled backwards, crushing Konrad beneath him. A great cry went up from the crowd, for it surely looked like both horse and rider were dead!

But to their amazement, Konrad crawled out from under Kurfurst, and spoke gently to his up-ended horse, which then sprang to its feet. Konrad remounted and, with all the cool courage of a true hero, completed the rest of the course without a single fault. Needless to say, Germany won the gold medal!

OLYMPIC SIZZLER!

Before the eighteenth century, country types on horseback used to gallop over vast open fields chasing foxes. However, when fields were enclosed by fences after parliament's "enclosures" act, they were forced to start jumping over them. Not long afterwards, the sport of "show jumping" began.

4 FIGHT!

GETTING IT OUT OF YOUR SYSTEM

Amongst its many other excellent benefits, sport can be a healthy outlet for the aggression that most human beings normally keep bottled up. This particularly applies to the group of Olympic events known as "combat" sports, many of which are based on skills used in warfare in days gone by.

Combat-related Olympic events include...

Archery: The object of Olympic archery is to shoot arrows from a bow as closely as possible to the centre of a target known as a "bull's eye". (Please note, you should never shoot an arrow at a real bull's eye, or anyone else's, for that matter.)

Fencing: In Olympic fencing, participants try to touch each other with the tips of their swords (or build barriers around gardens).

Boxing: In Olympic boxing, the combatants punch each other to try and score points or to knock out their opponent.

OLYMPIC SIZZLER!

At the 1900 Paris Olympics, live pigeons were actually used in the shooting event. Three hundred birds were released and Belgian Leon de Lunden won gold when he shot 21 of them, (imagine if the survivors had then taken their revenge by "carpet-bombing" him).

Shooting: Olympic shooting events involve guns such as pistols, rifles, shotguns and rocket-launchers. In all of the events you shoot at "still" or "moving" targets and are awarded points for accuracy.

Taekwondo: This sport originated in Korea and is a kind of unarmed combat designed solely for self-defence. A loose English translation of the word "taekwondo", is "the way of the hand and the foot", i.e. how to use your hand or foot to disable an attacker.

Judo: Judo is a Japanese word meaning "gentle way". It involves participants hurling their opponents to the floor, painfully twisting their legs and arms, hitting them with their hands and feet and using strangle holds known as the "chokes", (but of course, all, really, really gently).

How to be an Olympic Wrestler

There are two sorts of Olympic wrestling: Freestyle and Greco-Roman. Greco-Roman is based on the wrestling which took place at the ancient Olympic Games at the Hippodromus, and its rules forbid you to use your legs to bring down your opponent or to hold them below the waist. If you can't find any ancient Greeks or Romans to wrestle you'd be best to go for freestyle wrestling. Here's how to do it...

FREESTYLE WRESTLING: THE GENERAL IDEA

1 Most freestyle wrestling matches last for three, two-minute rounds (or about two seconds if you're rubbish!).

2 To win the match, you must "pin down" your opponent's shoulders for one second, (this doesn't mean you have to use enormous pins to hold them down… this would result in a court appearance).

3 You can also win your freestyle Olympic wresting match by "throwing" or "take down" moves. Each move you make will earn you points if you do it well. And you need three points to win the match.

4 If neither of you are awarded three points nor manage to pin down your opponent, the match goes into an "overtime" period. The wrestler who receives most points during overtime is the winner.

OLYMPIC SIZZLER!

At the Stockholm Olympics in 1912, a wrestling bout between Martin Klein of Russia and Alfred Asikainen of Finland went on for an exhausting 11 hours and 40 minutes, before Klein finally won by pinning down his opponent.

LET'S WRESTLE: WHAT YOU NEED

IF YOU WERE AN OLYMPIC WRESTLER, YOU WOULD NEED THESE THINGS...

A **A singlet:** this stretchy, one-piece garment is designed to prevent you and your opponent from carrying out any sneaky moves. For instance, if you were wearing shorts your opponent might unsportingly grab you by the waistband and lift you high into the air, causing you great discomfort and embarrassment.

B **Light and flexible wrestling shoes,** definitely no steel-toed pit boots or cowboy boots with spurs.

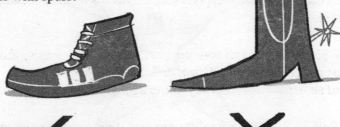

C **A handkerchief:** you tuck this into your singlet and use it to wipe blood from your wounds and mop up the wrestling mat if you happen to "leak" during the bout. Yuck!

D **A helmet** (optional) to protect you from getting a cauliflower ear (when your ear gets all big and lumpy after being hit), not to mention asparagus-lip and carrot-mouth.

ON THE MAT: WHAT TO DO

1 When your name and your opponent's names are called you must stand at opposite corners of the mat (and pull terrifying faces at each other).

2 Walk forwards to meet your opponent and the referee in the centre of the mat.
Important: On no account must you wrestle the referee. Nor must you ask him to help you to wrestle your opponent. He is there to ensure the match is fought safely and fairly.

3 The referee will now inspect your singlet, headgear and shoes to check they are legal (and to ensure that you are not carrying any hidden weapons such as swords, brass knuckles or baseball bats).

4 Shake hands with your opponent. Whilst doing this, you must not attempt to bend back their fingers or squeeze their hand so hard so that they cry out in agony.

5 Begin wrestling using different wrestling moves to pin your opponent to the mat. Turn the page for a selection of Olympic wrestling moves.

Olympic Wrestlers: Know Your Moves

Ankle lock: This move doesn't involve attaching an actual padlock to your opponent's ankle. Simply grab their ankle, place it in the crook of your elbow, grab their toes with your other hand, then force them onto their back, twisting their foot to force their shoulders to the ground.

Leg lock: Tip your opponent onto their stomach then sit on their bottom. Grab one of their legs below the knee and keep pulling it towards your body until they surrender.

Head lock: Get behind your opponent and wrap your arms around their head. Grasp one of your arms with the opposite hand and pull hard.

Suplex: Grasp your opponent around the waist with both arms, lift them up then fall on top of them, (or just throw them at the referee).

Leg sweep: Grab your opponent around the chest and "sweep" their leg from under them with one of your legs, thrust your body forward as you do so that they fall onto the mat (and give them a vicious Chinese burn – optional).

THE ETIQUETTE OF WINNING

1 If you've won, the referee will halt the match by telling you to stop wrestling (or by throwing a bucket of cold water over both of you).

2 Shake hands with your opponent, your opponent's trainer, your opponent's manager, your opponent's sister, your opponent's hairdresser, the referee, the referee's mum, the photographers and, of course, every single one of the spectators.

3 The referee will now raise your arm in the air to declare you the winner (then whirl you around his head and hurl you into the crowd).

DID YOU KNOW?

If an ancient Greek boxing match was going on too long, the boxers took turns to stand totally still while their opponent used them as a punch bag until one of them was knocked out. This thrilling finale was known as a "klimax", a word people still use to do this day (but only if they're rubbish at spelling).

5 BIKE DREAMS

PEDAL FOR A MEDAL

In the Olympic cycling events, men and women wear the tightest clothes known to humankind. They also wear the brightest and most hideously coloured outfits known to the intelligent universe. Indeed, their clothing is so bright that the racers have to wear sunglasses just so that their fantastically bright and tight clothing doesn't blind them!

CYCLING EVENTS INCLUDE:

Track cycling: Track events take place on specially constructed banked raceways known as velodromes. Team and individual events include sprints, endurance races and pursuits (in which the riders race after people who owe them money).

Mountain biking: In which competitors must transform themselves into the cycling equivalent of a mountain goat as they negotiate rocky tracks, dizzying descents, exhausting climbs (and the Olympic car park).

Road cycling: Where Olympic cyclists ride along ordinary roads competing in time trials and races (whilst ignoring red lights, scattering pedestrians, pulling faces at car drivers and going the wrong way up one way streets).

BMX biking: In BMX events, the riders whizz around a series of jumps, bumps and tightly banked corners known as "berms", performing such dare-devil stunts as bunny-hops, tabletops and abubacas (which many of them can do, but can't actually say). Bicycling acrobatics fall into three groups:

Peg grinds: In which the rider slides along a surface on the axle pegs (metal pegs that stick out from the middle of the front and back wheels) of their bike.

Air tricks: Which take place in mid-air and involve somersaults, wheel spins and generally death-defying (or at least, broken-bone-defying) leaps.

Flatland tricks: Which, as the name suggests can be performed on the street as well as on a specially designed course, and often involve balancing on one wheel.

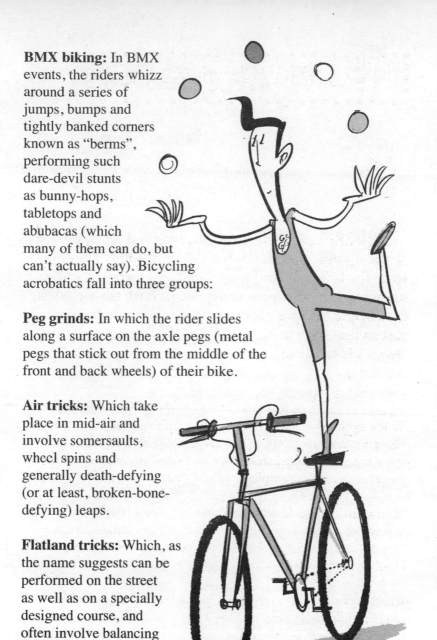

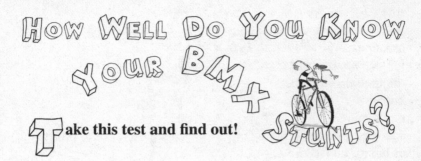

How Well Do You Know Your BMX Stunts?

Take this test and find out!

1 **What is a "bunny hop"?**
a) jumping the bike into the air from flat ground
b) bouncing the bike over rows of terrified rabbits
c) bouncing the bike over rows of hot-cross buns

2 **What is a "tabletop"?**
a) the contestant rides across a series of restaurant tables destroying people's dinners
b) the rider turns the handlebars and uses their body to make the bike look flat, like the top of a table
c) the rider balances on top of a flat surface without moving

3 **How would you describe a "pogo"?**
a) a move so frightening the rider has to rush to the toilet straight after performing it
b) swinging the bike onto its rear wheel whilst "hopping it" to maintain balance
c) swinging the bike onto its rear wheel then hopping it to the toilet

4 **What is a "nose manual"?**
a) where the rider steers the bike using just their nose
b) a move in which the rider stands on the bike's saddle in order to peer into people's gardens
c) where the rider balances the bike on its front wheel only without pedalling

5 When the rider hangs the rear of their bike over the opposite side of a ledge is it known as...
a) a toothpick hangover
b) a tail twister
c) a dental implant

6 When the rider brings their foot over the bike to the other side is it know as...
a) a can-can
b) a leg-over
c) a big mistake

7 When the rider uses the front brake to lift the back wheel and balance on the front tyre, is it known as...
a) a traffic violation
b) an endo
c) an innuendo

8 When the rider extends both feet outwards mid-jump to resemble a superhero, it's called a...
a) a Superman
b) a Spiderman
c) a Flying Sausage

6 HALF TIME: WHAT HAPPENED NEXT?

Olympic events can be very unpredictable. A combination of humans pushing themselves to their physical and mental limits, unforeseen circumstances and huge pressure can lead to all sorts of surprising incidents, and occasionally, unwelcome disasters. See if you can choose the right ending for the following Olympic true tales:

1 It was the Amsterdam Olympics of 1928. Henry Pearce was in the lead in his rowing race when he spotted a mother duck and her family of tiny ducklings directly in his path. What happened next?

a) Henry rowed on, scattering the ducklings and snatching several of them out of the water as he passed them. On winning the race, he celebrated with a slap-up dinner of "duckling à l'orange".

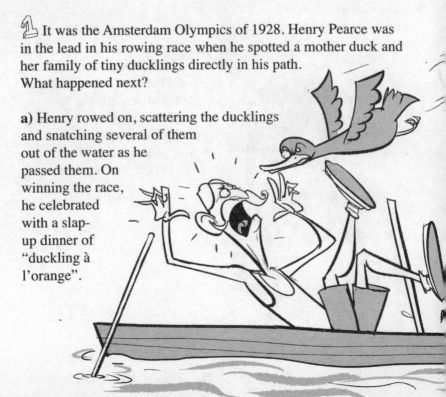

b) Spotting Henry, the enraged mother duck flew at him, hitting him with such force that he was knocked out of his boat and drowned.

c) Henry stopped rowing and waited until the ducks were clear. As he did, a French opponent overtook him and pulled away to a five-length lead. Nevertheless, Henry still managed to win the race, achieving hero status with the school children of Holland.

2 Australian competitor Edwin Flack was in the lead in the Athens Olympic marathon of 1896, confident of victory. However, just a few kilometres from the finish, he suddenly collapsed! Edwin's trainer asked a spectator to support the delirious athlete while he went to get a blanket. What happened next?

a) Thinking that he was being attacked, Edwin punched the helpful spectator in the face, and then passed out.

b) Suddenly reviving, Edwin and went on to win the race in record time with the helpful spectator slung over his shoulder.

c) Hardly able to believe his eyes, Edwin recognised the spectator as his long lost father, who was believed to have perished at sea many years earlier.

3 It was the 1956 Melbourne Olympics and a group of
students, led by a chap called Barry Larkin, felt rather
cheesed-off by all the official malarkey associated with the
games, so they decided to play a trick on the organisers.
What happened next?

a) Barry disguised himself as a hammer thrower. Wielding
what looked like an Olympic hammer, but was actually a black
balloon filled with mud, he hurled his hammer out onto the
field, causing utter confusion.

b) Barry and his pals built themselves a rather "special" boat
and took it down to the river where they "competed" in the
Olympic rowing race. However, rather than taking to the water,
they ran along the riverbank, their legs sticking out of the boat.

c) Barry and his mates made an "Olympic torch" out of an old
broomstick and a tin can which they painted silver then stuffed
with a pair of blazing underpants. Next, Barry raced through
Sydney several miles ahead of the real torch bearers. He
completely fooled the crowds and officials, who all cheered him
and his blazing Y-fronts to the skies.

4 Barcelona 1992. During the 400 metres race, Derek
Redmond collapsed in agony, his hamstring torn. Seconds later,
the Red Cross Ambulance team were racing towards him with a
stretcher. What happened next?

a) Determined to continue his race, Derek refused the team's
offer of help and crawled the last 250 metres to finish his race.

b) The Red Cross men lifted Derek onto the stretcher then raced
for the finishing line with their patient. However, they failed to
notice that they'd actually dropped Derek at the final bend and
crossed the finishing line with an empty stretcher.

c) Staggering to his feet, Derek began to hobble towards the finishing line. Seeing his son in agony, Derek's dad rushed onto the track and supported him for the rest of the race. Minutes later, Jim let go of Derek and his son finished unaided, the crowd cheering him to the rafters.

🖐 During a boxing match between Korean Byun Jong-il and Bulgarian Alexander Hristov at the 1988 Seoul Olympics, Byun repeatedly used his head as a battering ram. When the referee, Keith Walker, penalised Byun, Byun's trainer thumped Keith and the Korean fans began throwing chairs at him. Security guards were called. What happened next?

a) Seeing that Keith was in mortal danger, Byun, the head-butter, put himself between Keith and his attackers, saving the referee's life.

b) One of the security guards aimed a kick at Keith's head while the Chief of Security took off his uniform and chased him around the arena.

c) The fans knocked the security guards aside then began pelting Keith with rotten tomatoes.

7 STRETCH YOURSELF

BENDY, BOUNCY, BRILLIANT!

Gymnastics are fantastic to watch. In these awesome events, stunningly supple, skillful, strong and superbly coordinated athletes perform all sorts of breathtaking moves, including jaw-dropping jumps, somersaults and terrific twists and turns.

THESE ARE THE THREE CLASSES IN THE OLYMPIC GYMNASTIC SECTION:

Artistic: in which incredibly bendy people spring, swing, twist, dangle, bounce and balance on all sorts of apparatus including parallel bars, beams, pommel horses and rings.

Trampoline: in which incredibly bendy and bouncy people do all sorts of somersaults and twists, sometimes springing as high as 10 metres (risking getting their heads stuck in the ceiling).

Rhythmic gymnastics: a female-only discipline in which girls and women move rhythmically and elegantly whilst doing graceful things with ribbons, balls, clubs, hoops (wheelbarrows, bin lids and lawn mowers).

WHAT A HERO!

During the 1976 Montreal Olympics, Japanese gymnast, Shun Fujimoto, broke his knee during the floor exercise. However, despite being in total agony, he went on to score 9.5 on the pommel horse and 9.7 on the rings. He then dropped eight feet to the ground from the rings and still kept his balance after landing on his feet. Next, he raised his arms in a perfect finish before collapsing, having now also dislocated his broken kneecap and torn ligaments in his right leg. His team won the gold medal.

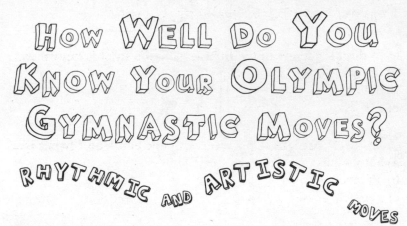

How Well Do You Know Your Olympic Gymnastic Moves?

Rhythmic and Artistic Moves

1 Balancing on one foot with your other leg high in the air and your chest up is called...
a) an arabesque
b) an Ali Baba
c) an ancient Egyptian

2 Sitting with your legs together straight in front of you with your body bent forward is known as...
a) a carp
b) a pike
c) a tadpole

3 Performing a turn on a vertical axis either on your feet or in a handstand is known as...
a) a pirouette
b) a pirate
c) a piglet

4 A jump to grasp the bar followed by lifting your legs and body up to the bar is known as...
a) a snooze
b) a kip
c) a kipper

TRAMPOLINING MOVES

6 A double somersault with at least half a twist is known as...
a) a fluffy
b) a fliffus
c) a frisbee

7 A single straight somersault with one and a half twists is...
a) a Rudolph
b) a Prancer
c) a stretcher case

8 A double back somersault with one and a half twists is known as
a) a thriller
b) a miller
c) a killer-diller

9 A single front somersault with three and a half twists is known as
a) a Rasputin
b) a Putin
c) an Adolph

10 A forward somersault with a half twist is called...
a) a biryani
b) a barani
c) an onion bhaji

8 THE 'ATHLONS

TRI', PENT', HEPT' AND DEC' (BUT NO ANT)

THE MODERN PENTATHLON was invented by Baron Pierre de Coubertin. It's based on the five skills a cavalry officer might have to rely on when delivering a really important message (or half a dozen pizzas) to his comrades out in the field, namely: riding, fencing, swimming, running and shooting (at the rotters who are trying to steal the pizzas).

THE DECATHLON consists of ten track and field events including the 110 metre hurdles, discus throw, shot put, pole vault and 400 metres running race.

THE HEPTATHLON is like the decathlon but for people who "tire out" more easily, as it only consists of only seven track and field events.

THE TRIATHLON is the simplest of the 'athlons, as it only consists of three events, (and is designed for people who can only hold a few thoughts in their head at any one time).

Nevertheless it is no less gruelling than the other contests, as you will now discover…

How to Win the Olympic Triathlon

When you take part in an Olympic triathlon you swim, then cycle and finally, run (then limp, to the first aid tent). In the most Olympic triathlon events, competitors have to do a 1,500 metre swim, a 40 kilometre bike ride and a 10 kilometre run.

Usually around 50 men and 50 women take part in each event with the aim of completing their triathlons in the shortest times (and briefest shorts) humanly possible.

The Triathlon: Be Prepared!

To make it as an Olympic competitor, you'll need different outfits for the different stages of your triathlon.

In the swimming section, you'll wear a wetsuit, for the cycling part you'll need a helmet and cycling shoes (a bike might also come in handy), and in the running stage, you'll wear running shoes (but not just running shoes, this isn't ancient Greece).

However, here's the good news: as it could have a negative affect on your performance, you don't actually have to carry your bike and all your other gear with you while you're doing the swimming bit of the triathlon. Instead, you will be given your own little area where you can store your gear and carry out your changes, or "transitions", as they're known.

Are You Ready Yet?

This may come as a bit of a shock, but in the triathlon, as well as timing your actual swimming, cycling and running stages, the Olympic officials will also be timing your transitions.

So, if you're an absolutely brilliant athlete who can swim like a fish, run like a cheetah and cycle like you're jet-propelled, but still haven't learned to tie shoelaces, do up buttons or take off your jumper without getting your head stuck in the neck-hole, you'll be in big trouble.

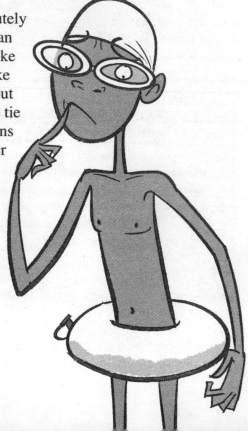

TRAINING FOR TRANSITIONS

Top triathlon athletes can do their first "transition" in less than a minute and their second in less than half a minute.

So, if you're going to stand any sort of chance of winning an Olympic triathlon medal, you really are going to have to carry out your transitions incredibly quickly!

And the best way to accomplish this is to rehearse them, whilst timing yourself doing it. Here are some tips for achieving record-breaking transition times. Don't forget, the clock is ticking!

TIPS FOR TRANSITION ONE: SWIMMING TO CYCLING

1 Prior to your triathlon, put your bike in the specially designated bike rack that forms part of your personal transition area. Make a mental note of where your transition area is. Don't forget there are 50 plus other triathletes competing and the rush to change over can be very chaotic.

2 Put your transition towel next to your bike and lay out your equipment in reverse order so that you'll pick it up in the order it's needed.

For Olympic triathlon transition success, attach your cycling shoes to the pedals of your bike with elastic bands and slip your feet into them while riding. As you pedal they'll snap and fall off (the elastic bands, not your feet).

3 Slap lots of Vaseline on under your wetsuit so that it will slide off really easily before you change into your cycling kit (but not that easily that it slides off while you're actually swimming).

4 As you're racing to your bike after the swim, save precious seconds by taking off your swimming cap and goggles and unzipping your wetsuit as you run.

5 Once you're on your bike and racing, pedal with your wet feet on top of your shoes then, when they're dry, slip them inside and fasten them.

6 HANDY HINT:

If you do wear cycling shorts don't wear underpants under them (especially those massive big ones that old people like to wear). If you do, the seams of your underpants will rub against all your bits and pieces while you're cycling and the friction will create sores (and also cause your bottom to ignite).

TIPS FOR TRANSITION TWO: CYCLING TO RUNNING

This is easier because all you have to do is take off your cycling helmet and change from your cycling shoes into your running shoes.

1 In advance, make sure you put talcum powder into your running shoes to prevent blisters, slacken the elastic laces slightly, leaving the tongue sticking out then lay them out in your transition area.

2 HANDY HINT:

Slip your feet out of your shoes while cycling up to the transition area and run in barefoot before putting on your running shoes.

3 WARNING:

When you start running expect your legs to feel really weird because of the change in activity.

Good luck. And don't forget, every fraction of a second counts!

9 CHUCKING STUFF AND JUMPING OVER THINGS

TRACK AND FIELD EVENTS

A whole heap of Olympic events date back to the days when human beings spent their entire lives:

1 Chasing after huge ferocious beasts

2 Throwing dangerous objects at huge ferocious beasts

3 Running away from huge ferocious beasts whilst leaping across ravines and over huge boulders.

These are known as track and field events because they take place on specially created tracks or the grassy areas of Olympic Stadiums.

TRACK AND FIELD EVENTS INCLUDE...

We'll come to the running events in the next chapter. In this one we're concentrating on the field events, starting off with...

OLYMPIC LONG JUMP: This is the event in which athletes try to jump as far as they can by racing up a runway then hurling themselves forward and landing in a sand pit (or the lap of an old lady sitting in the grandstand).

OLYMPIC HIGH JUMP: In this one, athletes try to jump as high as they can without the aid of poles (or enormous springs attached to the soles of their trainers).

OLYMPIC TRIPLE JUMP: This jump involves the athlete first hopping as far as they can, then skipping as far as they can, and finally jumping as far as possible forwards into a sand pit.

GRRR!

How to Throw the Olympic Hammer

If you were an Olympic athlete, and wanted to compete in the hammer-throwing event, you would need…

1 A hammer. Any old hammer won't do, nor will other tools such as screwdrivers, spirit levels or spanners. In days gone by, hammer throwers did actually throw a huge sledge-hammer, but now the "hammer" is actually a heavy metal ball attached to a wire and a handle.

2 Heavy duty hammer-throwing gloves. Throwers wear these to protect their hands, (thus avoiding their fingers actually "coming off" during their throw).

3 Smooth soled shoes (almost like bowling shoes).

4 A hammer-throwing cage. This looks like a really big bird cage made from a metal frame and netting. It's there to protect officials and spectators in case a hammer throw goes wrong, (FYI the hammer thrower stands inside the cage, not the officials and spectators).

5 The aim is to throw the hammer as far as possible without actually knocking over any officials or spectators or demolishing large buildings or national landmarks in the process. The best Olympic hammer throwers in the world achieve throws of more than 250 feet.

Did You Know?

After winning gold and silver medals at the 1972 Munich Games, American 400 metre runners, Vince Matthews and Wayne Collett were banned from the Olympics. Apparently, they had been "chatting" while the American national anthem was being played, not to mention "stroking their chins" and "twirling their medals" (oh, the shame of it!).

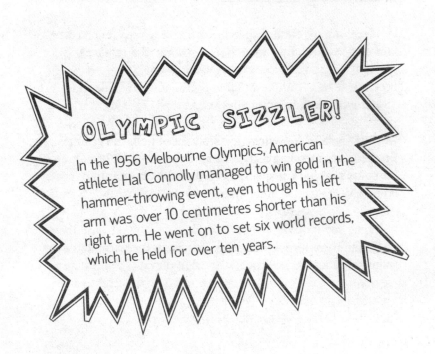

OLYMPIC SIZZLER!

In the 1956 Melbourne Olympics, American athlete Hal Connolly managed to win gold in the hammer-throwing event, even though his left arm was over 10 centimetres shorter than his right arm. He went on to set six world records, which he held for over ten years.

WHAT NEXT?

1 The thrower stands inside the throwing circle marked on the ground, whilst holding their hammer and looking really "up for it" and "well hard".

2 Taking a deep breath, the thrower then begins to "whirl" the hammer around in circles above their head (a bit like a medieval helicopter).

3 Once the hammer is really whizzing, they also begin to rapidly spin their bodies around in circles too, rather like a hammer-wielding spinning top.

4 Reaching maximum speed, the thrower now reaches the moment for which they have been training, the release!

There are several important factors athletes must take into account when letting go of a hammer:

A They must make a firm decision about how many times to spin their hammer and body around before letting go. Three or four spins is about right, but more than 300 is definitely not a good idea!

B It may seem obvious, but a thrower must make sure they release the hammer while facing the gap in the hammer cage, (easier said then done, especially when dizzy.)

BEWARE: LOW-FLYING HAMMERS!

At the Paris Olympics of 1900, the field events area was so small that the hammer throwers' hammers landed in the trees outside the stadium. The Swedish throwers hurled their hammers so wildly and erratically that spectators scattered in panic to avoid being clobbered by the missiles that hurtled towards them. And Hungarian discus thrower, Rudolf Bauer, managed to win the gold medal for his throws, even though three of them actually landed in the crowd.

THROWING THE JAVELIN

Javelin throwing was invented thousands of years ago by hairy people who had only just learned to walk upright. They did it so that they could they hunt deer, wild horses and woolly mammoths then turn them into food, tools, clothing (and elegant patio furniture).

Despite the fact that there are no more sabre-tooth tigers ready to pounce at any second, javelin throwing has evolved into a sophisticated Olympic sport.

HOW TO THROW A JAVELIN

Olympic javelin throwers train in the following way...

1 Most throwers (or at least the right-handed ones) hold the javelin horizontally in the palm of their right hand with the palm facing upwards. They choose one of the following grip styles:

a) American style: Gripping the javelin between the thumb and index finger

b) Finnish style: Gripping the javelin between the thumb and middle finger

c) Fork style: Gripping the javelin between the index and middle fingers

d) Neanderthal style: Gripping the javelin between their teeth

2 They hold the javelin high over their right shoulder with it aimed in the target direction, with the point slightly down.

3 Now they run towards the target line, accelerating smoothly (and not tripping over their shoelaces).

4 After taking about 12 strides, the thrower turns their left hip towards the target area so that their right leg crosses over their left.

5 At the same time they pull the javelin back with their throwing arm, keeping the javelin at shoulder height with their arm straight.

6 Launching their throwing arm forwards, as high as it will go and well ahead of their front foot, they must now release the javelin.

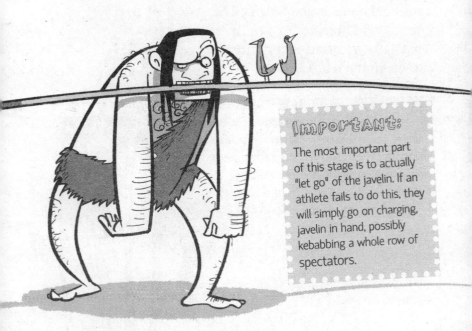

Important:

The most important part of this stage is to actually "let go" of the javelin. If an athlete fails to do this, they will simply go on charging, javelin in hand, possibly kebabbing a whole row of spectators.

THE POLE VAULT

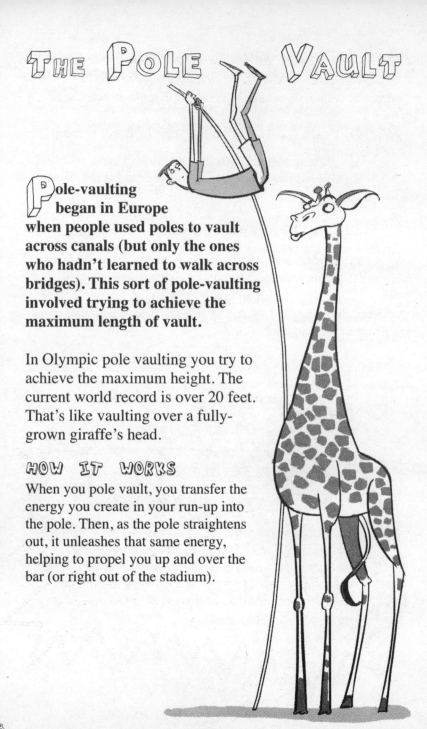

Pole-vaulting
   began in Europe
when people used poles to vault
across canals (but only the ones
who hadn't learned to walk across
bridges). This sort of pole-vaulting
involved trying to achieve the
maximum length of vault.

In Olympic pole vaulting you try to
achieve the maximum height. The
current world record is over 20 feet.
That's like vaulting over a fully-
grown giraffe's head.

HOW IT WORKS

When you pole vault, you transfer the
energy you create in your run-up into
the pole. Then, as the pole straightens
out, it unleashes that same energy,
helping to propel you up and over the
bar (or right out of the stadium).

HOW TO PERFORM A PERFECT "OLYMPIC CLASS" POLE VAULT

In order to vault over a very high pole, Olympic athletes need...

1 A really bendy vaulting pole made from layers of carbon fibre and fibreglass.

2 An all-weather track surface to run along.

3 A high bar to vault over.

4 A "box" for planting their pole in. It should be a sloping hole in the ground made from steel or aluminium.

5 A padded landing area made up of lots of big cushioned mats to ensure a safe and comfy landing.

6 Absolutely tons of courage! Although it looks like fun, pole vaulting is actually incredibly dangerous.

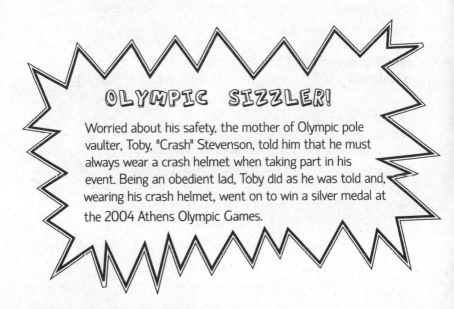

OLYMPIC SIZZLER!

Worried about his safety, the mother of Olympic pole vaulter, Toby, "Crash" Stevenson, told him that he must always wear a crash helmet when taking part in his event. Being an obedient lad, Toby did as he was told and, wearing his crash helmet, went on to win a silver medal at the 2004 Athens Olympic Games.

THE APPROACH:

1 The jumper (an Olympic athlete, not a knitted winter warmer) stands at the end of the runway holding their pole up horizontally.

2 They start with a slow run-up, preferably in the direction of the bar.

3 As they get closer to the take-off point, they lower their pole gradually, preparing to slide it into the box and start to increase their speed. The last two steps should be their fastest.

THE PLANT:

4 The pole must be slid or "planted" into the box, while the athlete has their arms stretched above their head.

5 Once the pole is successfully planted, the jumper leaps off the ground using their left foot, with their right knee up to drive themselves into the air. They are now transferring the energy of the run into the pole.

6 The pole should be sliding towards the end of the box and bending. Hopefully, the athlete should also be taking-off.

THE SWING-UP:

7 This is the hard bit. The jumper needs to swing their left leg up towards the top of the pole whilst keeping their right knee in the 90 degree "drive" position. They also have to "row" through quickly, using their bent pole, a bit like rowing a gondola. The rowing motion should keep the pole bent for as long as possible.

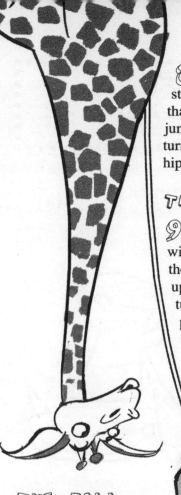

8 At this point, the pole will start straightening out again, releasing all that transferred energy to propel the jumper upwards. They will now be turning upside-down with their feet and hips above their head.

THE TAKE-OFF:

9 When they reach maximum height, with their body as straight as possible, the jumper drives their feet and hips up towards the bar and does a half turn to go over it, whilst releasing the pole so that it falls away from the bar and mats.

THE FALL:

10 Hopefully, the athlete will land on the mats. They don't try to land on their feet, as this is an easy way to sprain an ankle. Usually they land on their backs, facing up.

10 RUN FOR YOUR LIFE

OLYMPIC RUNNING

The Olympic Games involve lots of running races, and a few walking ones too (which have been specially included for really lazy athletes).

WHAT ARE THE SPRINTS?

The sprints are all the races under 400 metres (most of which are over so quickly that you wonder why they even bother in the first place).

Every year, some half human/half cheetah shaves another fraction of a second off the 100 metres world record (so, at some point in the future, someone will actually complete it in no seconds, (and accidentally travel back in time).

THE MYSTERY 100 METRES HERO

Unknown 100 metre runner, Percy Williams of Canada, astonished everyone by winning a gold medal at the 1928 Amsterdam Olympics.

Afterwards, a huge crowd of Canadians gathered outside Percy's hotel, hoping to catch a glimpse of their new hero. Spotting the crowd as he returned to his hotel, Percy joined them, eagerly awaiting the appearance of an Olympic superstar. D'oh!

STELLA THE SPEEDY FELLAH

One of the greatest female athletes ever, Stella Walsh, won a gold medal in the 100 metres at the 1932 Los Angeles Olympics and a silver medal in the same event in the 1936 Berlin Olympics.

In 1980, Stella was shot dead during an armed robbery. When her body was examined by doctors, they discovered that she was actually a "chap".

THE DISTANCE RACES

The distance races include the **800 metres** and the **1500 metres, and involve the athletes running around and around the running track whilst poking their elbows in other competitors' ribs as they "pace" themselves and prepare to make a "break" for the lead (as opposed to the nearest runner's leg).**

THE HURDLES

The hurdles, such as the 100 metres, are the races where the athletes jump over fences as they run.

DID YOU KNOW?

In the 1900 Paris Olympics hurdles event, runners had to jump over broken telegraph poles.

THE STEEPLECHASE

The steeplechase involves athletes running and leaping over lots of hurdles and water jumps (which the really small steeplechasers have to swim).

Steeplechases began in Britain when athletes raced from one town's steeple to the next town's steeple (then climbed it).

RACE WALKING

Olympic race walkers compete over distances of 20 kilometres and 50 kilometres, during which time they must always remain in contact with the ground. Medals are awarded to the first athletes to cross the line (and the ones who've been walking in the silliest way possible).

THE 4 × 100 METRE RELAY

In this Olympic sprinting event there are four athletes in each team. Each one runs 100 metres before handing over a "baton" to another team member, making sure they thrust it firmly into their hand, (and don't release it until they've been given a signed receipt).

OLYMPIC SIZZLER!

After sustaining an injury during the 1984 Los Angeles Olympics, Puerto Rico's Madeline de Jesus secretly got her twin sister Margaret to impersonate her in the 4 x 100 metre relay event.

THE MARATHON

The marathon was inspired by an event that took place after the Battle of Marathon in which a messenger ran all the way to Athens to announce the Greek victory, covering the huge distance of 42 kilometres, (whilst raising 10,000 drachma for his local *Help the Hoplites* charity).

Marathon running is an exciting and challenging Olympic sport with its own words and phrases. Take this test to find out…

HOW WELL DO YOU KNOW YOUR LONG-DISTANCE JOGGING JARGON?

1 What is adrenaline?

a) the line behind which all the runners must stand at the start of a race

b) a hormone which makes your heart rate increase, causing you to run faster

c) the first name of the record-breaking Swedish women's marathon champion, Adrenaline Bergman

2 What is "back-to-front" racing?

a) races where all the runners have to run backwards for the whole course

b) races where runners have to race in pairs with the entire front of one runner's body staying in contact with the entire back of their partner's body throughout the race

c) slowly working your way through the leading group of runners without actually going into the lead until the last few miles of the race

③ What are water stations?

a) places along the marathon route where runners can stop for a cold shower

b) places on the marathon route where runners are allowed to wee in people's front gardens

c) places where runners can get a drink of water

KEEP
ATHENS
TIDY!

What is chip timing?

a) running where a competitor's time is recorded by an electronic chip attached to their running shoe

b) races where Canadian Olympic gold medal winning marathon runner, Chip Butty, sets the pace for the first 24 kilometres

c) races where all the runners compete to see who can eat 15 bags of chips in the shortest time possible

5 What does "hitting the wall" mean?

a) what happens when a marathon runner isn't looking where they're going

b) the point in a marathon where the body's energy supplies become used up

c) what some slightly bonkers, frustrated and angry runners do if they haven't achieved their target race time

6 What is "fartlek"?

a) training which involves eating huge amounts of baked beans then being jet-propelled by the "thrust" of escaping gas

b) training at different speeds and intensities of running

BRRP!

c) the second name of the German record-breaking men's marathon champion, Horst Fartlek

7 What is "jogger's nipple":

a) a huge water fountain from which runners traditionally drink before marathons

b) sore and bleeding nipples caused by them constantly rubbing against your shirt as you run

c) a situation common in major marathons where some very unlucky runners' nipples actually drop off during the race and are later swept up by street cleaners.

THE MIND-BOGGLING ST LOUIS MARATHON OF 1904

The marathon course began and finished in the Olympic stadium in St Louis, Missouri. In between there were 42 kilometres of dusty roads, hills and incredibly hot temperatures, yet the first water-stop was 20 kilometres from the start of the race.

Fred Lorz quickly took the lead but, after 14 gruelling kilometres, he collapsed with agonising cramps.

Cuban postman, Felix Carvajal, had raised money to attend the Olympics by running around the central square in Havana. However, on reaching America he gambled away all his money and had to hitchhike to St Louis. He arrived with nothing but the clothes on his back: working boots, a beret, a long shirt and long trousers.

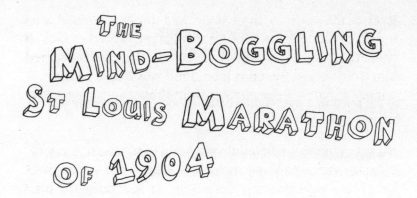

Taking pity on Felix, someone "trimmed" his shirt and cut off his trousers at the knees. So, in his snazzy new "shorts" and "singlet", he thundered along with the rest of the runners, overtaking the collapsed Fred.

Back at the stadium, three hours and thirteen minutes after the race had begun, a lone figure charged onto the track. It was Fred, the runner who'd collapsed. The crowd cheered him to the skies. Seconds later, Fred was declared the winner and posed for pictures with President Roosevelt's daughter.

However, before he could collect his gold medal, a cry of, "Cheat!" rang out. Someone had spotted Fred getting into a car! Fred immediately "fessed-up" to accepting the lift, and was banned from ever entering a marathon again.

So who did win? Not Cuban postman Felix, who finished fifth, despite having stopped to pick some apples and chat to spectators along the way.

The answer is Thomas Hicks. With ten miles to go, Thomas collapsed from heat exhaustion, but after being given some strychnine (a poisonous substance, often used to kill rats), he was off again.

Next he suffered from hallucinations, and was given yet more strychnine and brandy! By the time he reached the stadium, he could hardly stand up, and was unable to collect his medal because he was now 95 per cent dead.

It was only due to the efforts of four doctors that he survived. He never ran again (wonder why?).

11 THE REALLY SWEATY STUFF

Some Olympic events don't fit neatly into categories such as running or cycling, so we've bundled this lot into a bunch of activities that generally get athletes pouring with sweat (and if they aren't then they ought to be thoroughly ashamed of themselves).

WEIGHTLIFTING

Using two methods known respectively as the "clean and jerk" and the "snatch", Olympic weightlifting contestants attempt to lift the heaviest weights possible without bursting a blood vessel, falling over or actually "exploding" and showering spectators with their bodily bits and pieces.

The "snatch" consists of the lifter raising the weights above their head in one smooth, unbroken movement, while the "clean and jerk" consists of two movements, the first to the chest area and the second above the head.

AAARGH!

Weightlifting is definitely for tough guys. During the 2008, Beijing Olympics, Hungarian weightlifter, Janos Baranyai had just started to lift his 148 kilogram weights, the equivalent of lifting two huge men above his head, when disaster struck.

At a crucial moment, his elbow, no longer able to support the barbell, suddenly popped right out of its socket, in effect, turning itself back-to-front. In the next instant, Janos was on the floor shaking all over and screaming in agony!

BALL GAMES

BASKETBALL

In Olympic basketball two teams of five really tall people try to a shoot a ball into their opponents' net or basket.

THE HISTORY OF BASKETBALL

Basketball was invented in 1891 by a teacher who wanted to distract a very badly behaved class from becoming even naughtier during the winter, when the snow kept them indoors. He fastened peach-picking baskets to three-metre high railings and got the kids to shoot soccer balls into them. Every time a player scored, they had to climb a ladder to retrieve the ball from the basket.

DID YOU KNOW?

Believe it or not, it took over twenty years for someone to finally come up with the idea of putting a hole in the bottom of the basket so that the ball would drop straight through!

VOLLEYBALL

I n Olympic volleyball two teams of six players separated by a net attempt to "ground" a ball (make it hit the floor) on their opponents' side of the net. The players are allowed to strike the ball with any part of their body.

However quite sensibly, they mainly use their hands and arms, as hitting a ball with some of your other bits is often painful and ineffective.

BEACH VOLLEYBALL

Beach volleyball is much the same as indoor volleyball except that the teams have only two players and it's played on a beach, or on a heap of sand near Trafalgar Square.

FOOTBALL

Football is the most popular sport in the world. Points are awarded to the teams with the most speeding points on their driving licences, ridiculous hairstyles and, biggest, shiniest cars.

THREE ESSENTIAL SKILLS FOR ASPIRING OLYMPIC FOOTBALLERS

1 SHIRT PULLING

Constant failure to intercept
players, gain possession
of the ball, or play any
part in the game at all,
can be remedied by this
simple strategy.

First, having ensured that the ref' is
not looking, grab hold of your nearest
opponent's shirt and tug at it like
a police dog catching a burglar. It
doesn't matter if the player doesn't
happen to actually have possession of
the ball, just don't get caught.

If you are spotted, perhaps by a linesman,
walk towards the referee with your arms
outstretched and your palms raised, gaping at them in
open-mouthed amazement that anyone should think that
you could stoop to such low, unsporting behaviour.

2 FALLING OVER AND PRETENDING TO BE HURT

This is also known as "taking a dive". Even if no players from the opposite team are within five metres of you, crash to the ground and begin writhing in agony, whimpering and holding whichever bit of your anatomy takes your fancy whilst pointing accusingly at the nearest opposing player.

If your acting is sufficiently convincing, you will be awarded a free kick, which is possibly the only time you will touch the ball during the entire match. Of course, you must not take the free kick until your team coach has treated your "horrendous" injury with the magic spray, which will instantly and miraculously make it better.

3 CELEBRATING A GOAL

If you do happen to put the ball in the net you must punch the air, then raise your arms to a horizontal position and run the entire length of the pitch pretending to be an aeroplane.

When you reach the opposite end of the "park", fall on your knees and skid along the grass whilst lifting up, or even ripping off, your shirt. Next, your team-mates must pile on top of you and you must all roll around like toddlers in a sand pit.

However, they must take great care not to crush you to death, as this would result in them playing the rest of the match with only ten men.

12 COMPLETELY BATTY!

BAT AND BALL GAMES... WHERE DID THEY BEGIN?

Ten thousand years ago, a couple of prehistoric people carrying wooden clubs began batting wildly at a giant hornet that wouldn't leave them alone... And so lawn tennis was born!

Or something like that, anyway. Ever since then, human beings have been dreaming up variations on this "hit a moving object at another person" theme, many of which have now become Olympic sports such as...

SQUASH

Squash is the high-speed Olympic racket sport in which two or four players leap around a walled-in court like hyperactive chimpanzees, as they attempt to hit a very squashy ball. Squash balls have small coloured dots on them to indicate their level of bounciness. These range from orange, which is not very bouncy at all, to blue, where you only have to look at the ball for it to begin pinging around the court like a deranged bee. There are all sorts of squash shots, many of which have extremely strange names such as the "kill", the "trickle boast", the "nick", the "skid boast", the "Philadelphia", the "Mizuki" and the "squeeze boast".

HOCKEY

Hockey is an Olympic sport in which two teams of eleven players, armed with walking sticks, occasionally knock a small hard ball into a net defended by a person wearing a mattress.

DID YOU KNOW?

Hockey sticks are always cheerful, hence the term "jolly hockey sticks". (Honest!)

LAWN TENNIS

Tennis is the Olympic racket sport in which points are awarded to the players who make the most alarming and unusual grunting, screaming, shrieking and roaring noises as they bounce around a patch of grass trying to hit a ball.

BADMINTON

This racket game is a bit like lawn tennis but instead of hitting a small yellow ball, the players instead attempt to wallop a cute little bundle of feathers called a shuttlecock.

TABLE TENNIS

Table tennis is also like lawn tennis but, rather than being played on grass, it's played on a small table painted green to resemble a lawn. However, you don't actually stand on the table to play the game. That would just be silly.

Also, on winning, you should avoid the temptation to leap over the net to shake your opponent's hand, (as they do in lawn tennis). Table tennis is a popular sport and, no doubt, you may well already have some experience of playing it.

But how well do you know your table tennis? Take this test and find out . . .

The Olympic Table Tennis Test

1 An essential part of being able to play table tennis well is having…

a) good footwork   **b)** nice hair   **c)** rich parents

2 Before a table tennis match starts the umpire inspects the players'…

a) bats   **b)** hats   **c)** pockets

3 What are "long pimples"?

a) the name for tall, spotty newcomers to the game

b) the nick-name given to 1930s Olympic table tennis ace Bertie "Long Pimples" Palmer

c) the longer stippled rubber surface on the face of a table tennis bat

4 **If a player "twiddles" during a match they…**
a) fiddle constantly with their hair in order to distract their opponent
b) accidentally wet themselves whilst returning a particularly difficult serve
c) turn their bat in their hand

5 **You must hit the ball over the net so that it lands…**
a) on your opponent's side of the table
b) in your opponent's pocket
c) in the umpire's garden

6 **Once the ball has bounced on your side of the table you must…**
a) hit it back
b) head it back
c) put it in your pocket and run away

7 **In order to score a point in table tennis you must…**
a) make your opponent cry
b) hit the ball so that your opponent is unable to return it
c) give the umpire five pounds

8 **Table tennis is also known as**
a) ping-pong
b) whiff-whaff
c) farty-flap doodle

9 **The rest period between games finishes…**
a) after one minute
b) after three weeks
c) when one of the players finally wakes up

10 A "kill" shot occurs when...

a) a player smashes the ball so hard that their opponent is unable to return it

b) a player smashes the ball so hard that it fatally injures their opponent

c) a player smashes the ball so hard that it is vaporised

11 If a table tennis player "floats" a shot they...

a) hit the ball so that it stops and hovers motionless in mid-air for several seconds before continuing

b) hit the ball so that it has no "spin"

c) blow on the ball while it is in mid-air so that it changes direction

13 JUST SPLASHING AROUND

DON'T BE A DRIP, GET WET!

Lots of Olympic sports involve getting wet. Some of them are held in the sea, others in rivers or specially constructed watercourses and others, such as swimming, water polo and diving, at purpose built aquatics centres. Here's a quick roundup of the main events:

DIVING

After climbing the steps of a dizzyingly high platform, competitors hurl themselves into the water headfirst in the most stylish way possible, (or climb back down again, having now realised just how high that platform is!). Dive styles involve positions such as the "straight", the "tuck" and the "pike" (in which the diver must return to the surface holding a large freshwater fish between their teeth). In the synchronised diving events, pairs of athletes dive in tandem (that's at the same time, not whilst riding a two-person bike).

WATER POLO

This event is a bit like playing handball in a lake. Two teams attempt to throw the ball into the opposition's goal without drinking too much swimming-pool water. Water

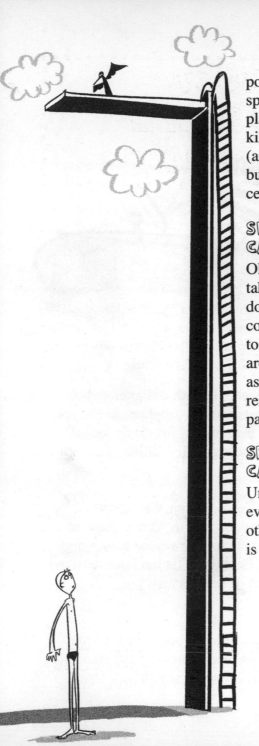

polo is an exhausting sport in which some players swim as far as five kilometres during a game (and then have to catch a bus back to the aquatics centre)!

SLALOM CANOEING

Olympic competitors take part in timed runs down a "white-water" course in which they have to negotiate their way around obstacles known as gates (which they must remember to close after passing through them).

SPRINT CANOEING

Unlike the white-water events, canoeists race each other on still water (which is usually blue).

SAILING

Olympic sailing involves people with designer stubble and sunglasses racing boats such as dinghies, keelboats, windsurfing boards (and pedalos) whilst doing lots of grinning and waving and occasionally falling in.

WHAT A HERO!

In the 1984 Olympics in Seoul, Korea, Canadian yachtsmen Lawrence Lemieux was in second place in a sailing boat race when he stopped to rescue a drowning Singaporean yachtsman. He came 21st but later received an award for his noble act of selflessness.

ROWING

Teams or single competitors propel boats through the water with oars as they race each other (or just stand on the river bank having massive arguments).

SYNCHRONISED SWIMMING

In this very demanding event, teams of swimmers perform graceful "synchronised" moves to music, some of them under the water and some of them on the surface. Moves have names like the "flamingo", the "side fishtail", the "crane", (and of course, the ever-popular, "dancing around your handbag").

SWIMMING

The four strokes used in Olympic swimming events are freestyle, backstroke, breaststroke and butterfly. Races include relays, 50 metres, 1500 metres and medleys, in which swimmers use all four styles in one race (but not all at the same time).

HOW TO BE A MEDAL-WINNING OLYMPIC SWIMMER

1 Practise Your Technique on Dry Land

No matter where you happen to be, on the bus, in the supermarket queue, school dinner hall or the dentist's waiting room, if you do have a few spare minutes, never miss an opportunity to strengthen your muscles and perfect your style.

2 Practise Your Technique in Water

You must perfect your strokes and build up your strength and stamina at every opportunity. Visit your local swimming pool as often as you can.

ON YOUR SHARKS, GET SET... GO!

When swimmer, Paula Bolopa, of Equatorial Guinea, was training for the 2000 Sydney Olympics, there were no swimming pools in her country, apart from one, in a private hotel.

The hotel management said she could practise in it, but only when there were no guests using it. The only other place she could train was in the sea, but this was dangerous because of sharks and treacherous tides. After her Olympic race she commented, "It's the first time I've swum 50 metres... it was further than I thought. I was very tired."

DID YOU KNOW?

At the 1900 Paris Olympics, underwater swimming was an Olympic event. However it was only held the once, possibly because there wasn't very much for the spectators to look at?

OLYMPIC SIZZLER!

When French swimmer Jean Boiteux won the 400 metres freestyle swimming race at the 1952 Helsinki Olympics, his dad was so chuffed that he leapt into the pool fully clothed so that he could him a great big hug! And you think you have an embarrassing dad!

SUPER-SLOW OLYMPIC HERO!

Also from Equatorial Guinea, Paula Bolopa's teammate, swimmer Eric Moussambani, was taking to the water. Like Paula, Eric also didn't have access to a swimming pool to train in, and had instead practised swimming in a crocodile-infested river!

When Eric Moussambani turned up for his heat, unlike his competitors, who looked very snazzy in their slick, black bodysuits, he had on a very ordinary-looking pair of blue swimming trunks. However, as his competitors were disqualified for a false start, Eric ended up racing himself.

"Piece of cake!" you may think. But remember, Eric had never swum in an Olympic pool before. Nor had he ever swum further than 50 metres. And now he was expected to complete 100 metres. To the cheers of 18,000 spectators, and with no one else in the pool, he managed his first length reasonably well. However, on his return, he suddenly ran out of steam and looked like he was about sink to the bottom of the pool.

Just as the Olympic lifeguards were preparing to dive in and rescue him, Eric mustered all his remaining reserves of strength and finished his race, recording the slowest ever Olympic swimming time. But he did come first!

Later on, he said, "My muscles were hurting. I had never been in a pool that big before, I was very scared," before very sportingly adding that it was only the crowd's cheering which kept him going. Eric later became known as "Eric the Eel" as a result of his outstanding efforts.

TIPS FOR OLYMPIC SWIMMERS

1 You must wear an Olympic regulation swimsuit. And you're not allowed to wear anything underneath or on top of your swimsuit. Even another swimsuit!

WHY NOT?

An extra swimsuit can help to compress your body and trap air, which makes you more buoyant, so it is illegal. When it was discovered that the Swedish swimmer, Therese Alshammar had worn two swimsuits, one on top of the other, at the 2000 Sydney Olympics, she was immediately stripped of her medals (but thankfully, not her swimsuits).

2 Blow your nose before your race. Nothing is more unsightly than the sight of a world-class swimmer powering through an Olympic pool with ribbons of bright green snot trailing behind them.

3 If you happen to have an extremely hairy body, a massive head of hair or an enormous fuzzy beard, you must shave it all off in order to cut down on "drag" in the water. Leaving just one stray hair could add a millionth of a nano-second to your time, thus depriving you of the gold medal.

4 If you are one of the very few people who happen to have webbed feet, (they do exist), you should make this clear to the officials at the start of the race, just in case they try to disqualify you for wearing flesh-coloured flippers.

5 Buoyancy aids such as floats, inflatable bananas, tyre inner-tubes, yellow plastic ducks and rubber arm rings are not allowed in Olympic swimming.

WHAT NOT TO DO AT AN OLYMPIC SWIMMING EVENT...

1 At the start of your race the referee will make a series of short blasts on their whistle. This is the signal inviting you and your fellow swimmers to remove your clothing before going into the water. However, please remember that "removing your clothing" doesn't include removing your swimming costume.

2 No matter how excited you are about taking part in your first Olympics you must not wee in the pool as you swim. This is not only unhygienic but also very off-putting for your fellow competitors.

3 Try not to drink the water as you swim. You may have managed to restrain yourself from tiddling, but other competitors, overwhelmed with the enormity of the occasion, may not have managed to maintain such immense self-control.

4 No matter how competitive you feel towards your rival swimmers, you must not do anything to affect their performance such as hitting them, swimming in and out of their lane, or deliberately splashing them.

5 If, at some point during the race, you suddenly find you've completely forgotten how to swim, do not throw your arms around the neck of a fellow competitor in an attempt to save yourself from drowning as it could seriously affect their performance.

14 THE "DO-IT-YOURSELF" OLYMPICS

Organising your own DIY Olympics is absolutely loads of fun. And it's a lot easier than it sounds. Of course, you'll have to leave out some events, such as the sailing, pole-vaulting, canoeing, boxing and shooting, but almost all of the others can be held in your back garden, local park, swimming pool or school playing field.

You can knock together some of the equipment you'll need or just borrow some PE equipment from your school. When your teachers, or even your parents, find out what you're up to, they'll be so impressed that they'll want to join in!

DESIGN YOUR OWN DIY OLYMPICS LOGO

This is the image that sums up what your games are about. It could be a design incorporating a sporty picture, or just an attractive pattern with the words "DIY Olympics" in the middle. Most Olympic logos have rings in them. These five coloured circles represent the five competing continents engaging harmoniously in a magnificent, fair-minded, sporting competition.

YOUR DIY OLYMPIC MEDALS

These magnificent trophies are an essential part of your "greatest show on earth" event and can quite easily be made from plastic container lids wrapped in silver, bronze or gold foil with a ribbon threaded through a hole in them.

And while you're at it, don't forget to make the "podium" on which the winners will stand as they proudly display their trophies. This can be something as simple as a chair and a couple of wooden boxes.

Your DIY Olympics Opening Ceremony

The 2008 Beijing Olympics opening ceremony involved 15,000 performers, lasted an exhausting four hours and cost an insane amount of money! But if your pocket money won't stretch to covering the expenses of hundreds of dancers, performers and athletes, don't worry!

You can put together a spectacular and moving opening ceremony for next to nothing. Remember, it's not what you spend, it's about your creativity, imagination and determination to come up with something really original and spectacular!

OPENING CEREMONY TIPS

1 The essential ingredients of an opening ceremony are music, sound effects, singing, dancing, speeches, smiling, crying, flag-carrying, marching around looking proud and waving.

2 You'll need an Olympic torch, which must first be carried by a relay of thousands of specially selected bearers across the country, then passed to a famous sporting celebrity who will light the Olympic cauldron.

However, rather than going to all that trouble you could just get your Gran to run around for a few minutes holding a sparkler.

OFFICIALS, JUDGES AND DIGNITARIES

Get some adults to judge and "officiate" at your games, awarding points for things like the gymnastics and show jumping. You'll also need to invite some "dignitaries", such as your head teacher, doctor, local policeman, chimney-sweep or school nurse plus of course, your rellies. One of the top bananas must also declare the games open, as the Olympic cauldron (otherwise known as the family barbecue, also lit by an adult of course) is lit with the eternal Olympic flame (or, in your case, the eternal Olympic sparkler).

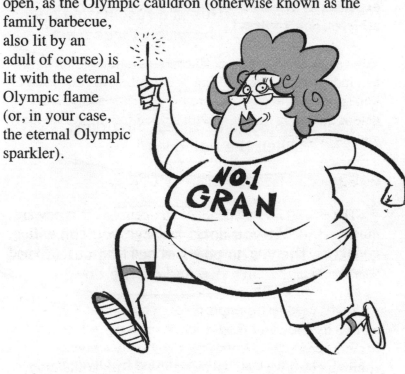

COMMENTATORS AND ANNOUNCERS

You'll need someone with a megaphone (or a really loud voice) to announce the events, and comment on them as they happen. As a general rule, try not to say things like...

"He dribbles a lot and the opposition doesn't like it. In fact you can see it all over their faces."

"This is a fascinating duel between three men!"

"There's going to be a real ding-dong when the bell goes."

"If you don't believe you can win, there's no point in getting out of bed at the end of the day."

...all of which have actually been said by Olympic commentators in the past.

The DIY Olympic Events

Most of your DIY Olympic sports can be organised with a bit of imagination and ingenuity, using bits and pieces you might find lying about in your house, garden shed or garage. Of course, you can't use *real* shot puts or javelins, that would be far too dangerous! Instead, here are some alternative suggestions...

Shot-putting: Use cabbages, pumpkins, grapefruit or melons as your "shot".

Javelin: Throw "mini javelins" (i.e. darts), at a dart board.

Weightlifting: Fill buckets with increasingly large quantities of water and see who can lift them the highest, one in each hand. You'll be surprised at how heavy they become.

Hurdling: Set up a series of jumps made with garden canes resting on upside-down buckets or chairs.

Discus: Use a frisbee as your discus and see who can throw it the furthest.

Show jumping: Use the same jumps as for the hurdles, but reposition them and get strong children, or strong adults, to take the part of the horses. Add in some "double hurdles" and a "water splash" made from a plastic paddling pool.

Trampoline gymnastics: If you've got a trampoline in your garden, you've no problems. Just get bouncing, Olympic style!

High jump: Use a garden cane balanced on a couple of upside-down dustbins or chairs with an old mattress or inflatable next to it for soft, safe landings.

Rhythmic gymnastics: Perform to music with hula hoops and lengths of ribbon.

Badminton and volleyball: Stretch a clothesline or a net between two posts or trees then mark out your court with string or flour.

Remember, these are just suggestions. You can no doubt come up with some really bright ideas of your own for the football, cycling, running and other events.

Your DIY Olympics Closing Ceremony

Your closing ceremony should be similar to your opening ceremony, but shorter (and with a lot more crying). As it ends, you must extinguish the Olympic flame (or in your case, the Olympic family barbecue), with the aid of a an adult and a big jug of water!

What Are You Waiting For?

After reading that lot maybe you're all fired up now and desperate to become an Olympic gold medallist! Well, it seems that you're almost never too young to start preparing for Olympic stardom.

And young hopefuls do go on to achieve Olympic glory. At the 1896 Athens Olympics a 10-year-old Greek lad finished third in the gymnastics' parallel bars.

In 1936, a 13-year-old American girl won the gold medal for springboard diving at the Berlin Olympics.

And in 1976, 14-year-old Romanian gymnast, Nadia Comaneci, won no less than three gold medals at the Montreal Olympics.

But That's The Awesome Olympics For You. Anything Can Happen!

GLOSSARY

AD All dates after the year that Christians believe Jesus was born, also known as **CE** (the Common Era)

adrenaline Hormone released by the body in high pressure situations

air tricks Tricks performed on a bike with no part of the bike or body touching the ground

agility Ability to move quickly and easily

athlete Person who takes part in sports, especially in competitive races

archery Sport which uses a bow and arrow to shoot at a specific target

badminton Sport which uses long-handled rackets to hit a shuttlecock (a cone shaped object with a rubber nose) back and forth over a high net

basketball Game where two opposing teams try and throw a ball through a three metre high hoop as many times as possible

BC All dates before the year that Christians believe Jesus was born, also known as **BCE** (Before the Common Era)

BMX Modified bike which is smaller and tougher than a traditional racing bike. BMX bikes are used for cross-country racing and performing tricks

boxing Sport where two opponents fight one another with their fists, wearing padded gloves

bunny hop Jumping a bike into the air from flat ground

chariot Two-wheeled horse-drawn cart used in ancient racing

decathlon Race consisting of ten separate events, for example, running, cycling, swimming etc.

dexterity Ability to perform tasks with skill

dignitary Person who is considered to be important

discus Heavy disc shaped object used in throwing events

dive To jump head first into water

DIY Stands for "do-it-yourself"

dolichos Distance race of between two and a half and five kilometres

embassy Place where an ambassador (a person sent from one country's government to another country) lives and works

entrails Animal or person's internal organs

equestrian Horse riding and other horse-related events

fartlek Training at different speeds and levels of difficulty

fencing Sport of fighting with swords

flatland tricks Tricks performed on a BMX bike from flat ground

football Game played by two teams in which the ball may not be touched by the arms or hands (known in the US as "soccer")

grapple Fight or struggle

gymnastics Form of exercise displaying strength, speed and coordination

hallucination Seeing something which is not there

hammer throw Sport where the aim is to throw a heavy metal ball as far as possible

heptathlon Race consisting of seven separate events

high jump Event where the aim is to jump over a raised bar without touching it

hippodrome Greek term for a horse racing course

hockey Game played between two teams using long, curved sticks and a small ball

hoplitodromos Ancient Greek Olympic foot race where the athletes wore amour

hurdles Race which involves jumping over obstacles

irreligious Lacking any religious faith

javelin Long thin spear thrown in competitive sports

judo Very physical sport in which athletes aim to unbalance their opponent

lawn tennis Game played with rackets where a soft ball is hit back and forth over a low net

linesman Official who assists the referee from the sideline

lithe Thin or graceful

long jump Event where the aim is to jump as far as possible

marathon Long distance running race

neurologist Doctor who deals specifically with the brain

nimble Fast and agile

nose manual Balancing a bike on its front wheel only without pedalling

officiate Someone who is in charge of a sporting event

pankration Ancient Greek sport similar to wrestling and boxing, but with less rules

peg grind Slide along a surface on the axle pegs of a BMX bike

pentathlon Race consisting of five separate events

pogo Swinging the bike onto its rear wheel whilst "hopping it" to stay balanced

pole volt Event where athletes use a long pole to help them jump over a raised bar

prehistoric Referring to a period in time before written records

pugme Ancient Greek form of boxing where leather straps are wrapped around the fists instead of gloves

rival Person that competes with another

shot put Sport where a very heavy round ball is thrown as far as possible

singlet All-in-one clothing worn during wrestling matches

slalom canoeing Canoeing down-river while avoiding obstacles

sophisticated Complex and advanced

sprint Short, fast race

squash High-speed game played with a hard rubber ball against a wall

stamina Ability to keep going for long periods of time

steeplechase Running race in which runners must clear hurdles and water jumps

synchronised swimming A team of swimmers perform identical movements in time to music

table tennis Indoor game based on tennis, played with small bats and a ball bounced on a table divided by a net

tabletop Jump where a bike rider turns the handlebars and uses their body to make the bike look flat, like the top of a table

taekwondo Korean martial art designed for self-defence

track cycling Bike racing events which take place on specially constructed raceways knows as "velodromes"

trajectory Path followed by a moving object

triathlon Race consisting of three separate events

triple jump Athletic event in which competitors attempt to jump as far as possible by performing a hop, a skip, and a jump from a running start

unaesthetic Not pleasing in appearance

velodrome Arena for track cycling

volleyball Game played by two teams where a ball is hit by hand over a high net

water polo Game played by two teams in a pool which involves throwing a ball into the opponent's net

weightlifting The sport of lifting heavy weights

FURTHER INFORMATION

BOOKS

Who's Who in Olympic History by Charlotte Guillain (A & C Black, 2008)
World Sports: BMX and Mountain Biking by Paul Mason (A & C Black, 2010)
The Paralympics by Nick Hunter (Wayland, 2011)
The Story of the Olympics by Richard Brassey (Orion, 2011)
History (The Olympics) by Moira Butterfield (Franklin Watts, 2011)
How the Olympics Came to Be by Helen East (British Museum Press, 2011)
Collins Big Cat: The Olympic Games by John Foster (Collins Education, 2009)
Big Match Manager by Tom Sheldon and Nathan Burton (Bloomsbury 2004)
Athletics, Field: Pole Vault, Long Jump, Hammer, Javelin and Lots, Lots More by Jason Page, (Lerner Pub Group, 2000)
Rush for the Gold: Mystery at the Olympic Games by John Feinstein (Knopf, 2012)
My Story: Berlin Olympics by Vince Cross (Scholastic, 2012)
Stadium School: Hot Prospect by Seb Goffe and Cindy Jefferies (A & C Black, 2008)

WEBSITES

Kidnetic
www.kidnetic.com

Change for Life
www.nhs.uk/Change4Life/Pages/change-for-life.aspx

BBC Ancient Greece: Olympic Games
www.bbc.co.uk/schools/primaryhistory/ancient_greeks/the_olympic_games

British Gymnastics
www.british-gymnastics.org

QuadKids Athletics
www.quadkids.org

Michael Cox
www.michaelcox.info

INDEX

adrenaline 86
Alshammar, Therese 112
Amsterdam 54–55, 83
Antwerp 21, 34
archery 42
armour 12
Asikainen, Alfred 45
Athens 16–17, 55, 86, 123

badminton 100, 122
ball games 94–97
Baranyai, Janos 92–93
Barcelona 23, 32, 56–57
Baron Pierre de Coubertin 16
basketball 94
bat and ball games 98–103
Bauer, Rudolf 75
Beijing 92–93, 118
Berlin 21, 40, 56, 83, 123
bike (see cycling)
BMX biking 51–53
Bolopa, Paula 108, 110
Bolt, Usain 35
boxers/boxing 8, 9, 11, 13, 14–15, 32, 42, 49, 57

canoeing 105
Carvajal, Felix 90–91
chariot races 8, 17
Collett, Wayne 73
combat sports 42–49
Connolly, Hal 73
cricket 18
cross country 36, 40
cyclists/cycling 23, 50–53, 63–69

discus throw 62, 75, 121
disqualified 32, 34
distance races 13, 84–85
diving 104, 123
dressage 36

endurance 30, 50
equestrian events 36–41
eventing 36
Eyser, George 19

fartlek 89
fencing 42
Flack, Edwin 55
football 95–97
freestyle wrestling 44–45

Gitsan, Charles 20
gloves 11, 17, 32, 72
gold medal 18, 19, 22, 35, 40, 43, 59, 73, 83, 123
golf 18, 33
Greco-Roman wrestling 44
Greece 8, 16–17
Greek gods/goddesses 8, 12
Guillemot, Joseph 34
Guttman, Sir Ludwig 22
gymnastics 19, 58–61, 119, 122, 123

hammer throwing 72–75

heat/heat exhaustion 22, 90–91
heptathlons 62
Hicks, Thomas 91
high jump 21, 23, 71, 122
Hippodrome 13, 44
hockey 99
horse racing/riding 13, 36–41, 62
Hristov, Alexander 57
hurdles 31, 62, 84, 121

injuries 10, 11, 32, 40, 46, 56–57, 59, 85, 93

javelin throwing 76–77, 121
Judo 43
lawn tennis (see tennis)
logo, designing 116
London 20, 22, 29, 34, 95
long jump 71
Lorz, Fred 90–91
Los Angeles 35, 83, 85
Lyon, George 33

Mallin, Henry 32
marathons 8, 17, 20, 33, 55, 86–91
McArthur, Kennedy 20
medal winning 18, 19, 22, 29, 35, 40, 43, 59, 66, 73, 79, 83, 112, 123
medals, designing 117
Melankomas of Karia 11
Melbourne 22, 73
Mexico 39
Milo of Kroton 11, 32
Montreal 59, 123
mountain biking 50
Moussambani, Eric 110–111
Munich 73
music 21, 22, 23

national anthems 21, 22, 73
Nike 12
nude 8

obstacle race 18
obstacles 18, 36, 38, 40, 105
Olympia 8
Olympic Games
ancient 8–15, 35, 44
first 8, 16
modern 16–23
Olympic torch 9, 118
opening ceremony 118–120

Pankration 13
Paralympics 22
Paris 18, 21, 75, 84, 109
Pearce, Henry 54–55
pentathlons 62
Periodonikes 12
podium 117
pole vault 62, 78–81
Pugme 13

Race walkers/race walking 22, 85
racket sports (see bat and ball games)
Redmond, Derek 56–57

referees 47, 49, 57, 96, 114
relay racing 9, 56, 85, 107
rhythmic gymnastics 58, 122
road cycling 50
rowing 31, 54–55, 80, 106
runners/running 8, 9, 17, 20, 33, 55, 56–57, 62, 63–65, 73, 82–91; (also see marathons)

sailing 106
Sakata, Toshiyuki 29
Seoul 57, 106
shooting 43, 62
shot put 62, 121
show jumping 36–41, 119, 121
silver medal 19, 29, 73, 79
singlet 46, 47
slalom canoeing 105
Sostratus of Sikyon 10
Spiridon, Louis 17
sprint canoeing 105
sprinters/sprints 17, 35, 50, 83, 85
squash 98
St Louis 19, 90–91
steeplechase 84
Stockholm 20, 33, 45
swimming 17, 18, 23, 34, 62, 63–66, 68, 105, 107–115
Sydney 108, 112
synchronised swimming 23, 107

table tennis 100–103
Taekwondo 43
tennis 17, 98, 100
Theo of Theagenes 14–15
Theodosius, Emperor 15
Tokyo 23
Toronto 23
track and field events 62, 70–71
training 11, 22, 35, 89
trampoline gymnastics 58, 122
transitions 64–69
triathlons 62–69
triple jump 71
tug-of-war 20

umpire 101
underwater swimming 109

volleyball 95, 122

Walker, Keith 57
Walsh, Stella 83
water polo 35, 104–105
weightlifters/weightlifting 22, 29, 92–93, 121
wheelchairs 22
white-water events 105
women 9, 16, 18, 21, 56, 58, 63, 83, 85, 108, 112
world records 73, 78, 83
World War II 22
wrestlers/wrestling 8, 10–11, 32, 44–49
wrestling moves 48